The Playboy of the Western World

The Playboy
of the Western World

J. M. SYNGE

with an Introduction by

T. R. HENN
CBE, MA, HON.LITT.D.(DUBLIN)

*Fellow of St. Catharine's College,
Cambridge. University Lecturer in
Poetry and Drama*

LONDON
METHUEN & CO LTD
11 NEW FETTER LANE · EC4

First published in this edition 1961
Reprinted 1964 and 1966
Introduction © by T. R. Henn
Printed in Great Britain
by the Shenval Press Ltd
London, Hertford and Harlow
1.3
Catalogue No. 02/6299/24

Contents

Introduction

Synge's work must be seen, at least in part, against the background of the Abbey Theatre and the ideas and ideals for which it stood. The history of the movement is complicated, both by politics and by personalities; yet we may attempt a brief sketch here. In 1891, W. B. Yeats had founded, in London, the Irish Literary Society, and in the following year the National Literary Society in Dublin. In 1893 the Gaelic League was founded by Douglas Hyde and others. Among its objects were the preservation and revival of the Irish language, the study of its existing literature, and the encouragement of a new literature to be written in Irish. Its effect was to produce a revival of many cultural traditions, a renewed national consciousness, which merged with the growing movement toward Home Rule and the 'de-Anglicization' of Ireland.

At an early stage members of the League had talked of producing plays in Irish; but, paradoxically, the first contribution came, in English, from the Anglo-Irish writers. In the years between 1892 and 1899 Yeats and others had discussed the possibility of opening a small theatre in Dublin: 'We hope to find, in Ireland, an uncorrupted and imaginative audience, trained to listen by its passion for oratory—we will show that Ireland is not the home of

7

buffoonery and of sentiment, as it has been represented, but the home of an ancient idealism'.[1] In 1899 an English company gave a season of Anglo-Irish plays in Dublin, and in 1902 the Irish National Theatre Society was formed.

It was a curious stroke of fate that threw together the promoters of the theatre. They included Miss Horniman, a wealthy Englishwoman from Manchester, who provided the financial backing; Edward Martyn, a Mayo land-owner, who knew a good deal about the theatre, but who was subject to a religious and sensitive conscience which rendered him unfitted to deal with the troubles that lay ahead; George Moore, also of landowning stock, liable to enormous and short-lived enthusiasms and with a great capacity for malicious anecdote. Above all there was Lady Gregory, the widow of a Clare landowner, who provided much of the practical business intelligence of the theatre, 'mothered' ceaselessly the frail and overworked Yeats, and made of her home at Coole Park both a *salon* where the great literary figures of the time could meet (so that Yeats could write of it in terms of Urbino and Castiglione's *The Courtier*) and a refuge for Yeats himself.

We must see, in the first instance, the new drama as in part a revolt against realism and the Ibsen-type drama; in part a rejection of the English commercial theatre of the last two decades of the century; in part a protest against a general Philistinism, to which Ireland, in her literary Renaissance, should provide a new opposing force. We must quote both Yeats and Synge on this matter:

'Why should we thrust our works, which we have written with imaginative sincerity and filled with spiritual desire, before those quite excellent people who

[1] From the Prospectus of The Irish Literary Theatre.

think that Rossetti's women are "guys", that Rodin's women are "ugly" and that Ibsen is "immoral", and who only want to be left in peace to enjoy the works so many clever young men have made specially to suit them? We must make a theatre for ourselves and our friends, and for a few simple people who understand from sheer simplicity what we understand from scholarship and thought.'[1]

Beside this we may set a passage from the Preface to *The Playboy*:

'In the modern literature of towns . . . richness is found only in sonnets, or prose poems, or in one or two elaborate books that are far away from the profound and common interests of life. One has, on one side, Mallarmé and Huysmans producing this literature; and on the other, Ibsen and Zola dealing with the reality of life in joyless and pallid works. On the stage one must have reality, and one must have joy; and that is why the modern intellectual drama has failed, and people have grown sick of the false joy of the musical comedy,[2] that has been given them in place of the rich joy found only in what is superb and wild in reality.'

There is, then, the revolt against the contemporary English theatre, of which Edward Martyn wrote slightingly on his return from France and Germany in 1899:

'The contrast has always struck me between the upholstered, drawing-room-like shapelessness of an

[1] W. B. Yeats, *Essays and Introductions* (1961), p. 166.
[2] We may perhaps think of the same contrast in Sir Philip Sidney's *Apologie*:
    'Delight hath a joy in it, either permanent or present. Laughter hath only a scornful tickling.'

9

English theatre, designed for an addled, over-fed audience, who loathe, above all things, any performance on the stage that would appeal to a lofty and aesthetic sense in humanity, and the grand lines and noble austerity of some foreign theatres like, let us say, the Théâtre Français, where the first consideration is not materialism but art.'[1]

The first performances of the Irish Literary Theatre were given at the 'Ancient Concert Rooms' in Dublin in 1899; in 1904 the Abbey was opened in a building of mixed character, partly the Mechanics' Institute and partly the old morgue. Many factors contributed to its success; one was a certain notoriety attending the production of Yeats' *Countess Cathleen*, which in 1899 had been violently attacked in the pamphlet called *Souls for Gold*, and which was produced later in the same year with police protection. Another was Yeats' discovery, in 1901, of two highly gifted amateur actors, William and Frank Fay; his discovery also of Florence Farr, who seemed in his view likely to popularize a new method of speaking verse[2]; and the consolidation of the Fay's Company into the new Society. Synge's contributions began in 1903, with *In the Shadow of the Glen*, followed in 1904 by *Riders to the Sea*, composed in that order. Then comes *The Well of the Saints* (1905), *The Playboy* in 1907, *The Tinker's Wedding* in 1908 (produced in 1909), and *Deirdre* (posthumously, with a preface by Yeats) in 1910.

Synge's contribution differed both from Yeats' proposed ideals and the general trend of the new movement. To Yeats one function of the theatre was to make the

[1] *cit.* Ellis-Fermor, *The Irish Dramatic Movement*, p. 27.
[2] *v.* 'Speaking to the Psaltery', *Essays and Introductions* (1961), p. 13.

nation conscious of its heritage in history and myth; to provide a point round which the popular imagination might first awaken and then concentrate its power; and at the last to unify itself for a nationalist effort by the imagery liberated in the drama. His plays were to be popular, not in the middle-class sense, but as representing *das Volk* and Gaelic culture, together with an epic national past. And thus the plays might serve, with this spiritual awakening, a political purpose; at the end of his life he was to ask, of the 1916 Easter Rising:

> '... Did that play of mine send out
> Certain men the English shot?'

By contrast, Synge's work is non-political, detached, ironic; interested in this excited yet dispassionate exploration of the world of the western peasantry, and of an imagination that was still 'fiery, and magnificent, and tender'. By 1909 the flame of his own life, and perhaps that of the first phase of the Abbey, had guttered and burnt out. An idealistic Nationalist movement had become entangled with politics and religion. Miss Horniman withdrew her support in consequence of the decision to open the theatre on the day of King Edward's funeral.[1] Edward Martyn withdrew his because of his conscience. The controversy over *The Playboy*, following that of *The Countess Cathleen*, exacerberated an already sensitive nationalism, which Shaw's *John Bull's Other Island*, and its *Preface*, had done little to mollify.

§ii THE PERSONALITY OF SYNGE

No biographical note is of any value, in a brief essay of

---

[1] We may parallel this with the banning in the Free State of the film of the Coronation of Elizabeth II.

this kind, unless it throws some light on the work itself. For our purpose we may note that Synge was born in a Dublin suburb in 1871, and therefore he was to grow up as a young man in the choking air of the '90s; contemporary with, but not among, those writers and poets of whom Yeats has written so vividly in *The Tragic Generation*.[1] His father was a Dublin barrister, who had some property in Co. Galway; his mother was the daughter of a rector in Co. Cork. On both sides, therefore, he was 'Protestant Ascendancy' by birth and tradition; the family was an ancient one, much connected with the Church. He went to Trinity College, Dublin, in 1888, and obtained prizes in Irish and Hebrew; one of his great interests was natural history, and he was a member of the Dublin Naturalists' Field Club. (The plays show an intimate knowledge of bird and beast, and some of the most vivid images are drawn from such sources.) But his main interest was music; and after leaving Trinity he spent some wandering years on the Continent, the Black Forest, Italy, France, presumably with the intention of becoming a professional musician. It is perhaps this aspect of the fiddler wandering over Europe that caused Yeats to align him in imagination with Oliver Goldsmith.

But his interests shifted from music to literature; Paris was then the centre of the great men, and of the younger English writers. (George Moore's *Confessions* give a spirited and often malicious picture.) After travel in Germany and France he appears to have settled in Paris; living in comparative poverty; talking incessantly with his friends, absorbing the life of Paris with something that may recall Keats' 'negative capability'. The account of

[1] *Autobiographies.*

12

Yeats' meeting with him in Paris (both were staying at a poor students' hostel in the Quartier Latin) is too famous not to quote:

> 'I said: "Give up Paris, you will never create anything by reading Racine, and Arthur Symons will always be a better critic of French Literature. Go to the Aran Islands. Live there as if you were one of the people themselves; express a life that has never found expression." I had just come from Aran, and my imagination was full of those grey islands where men must reap with knives because of the stones.'[1]

But what is of importance for our purposes is the European outlook that he had acquired in Germany, Italy, France; his assumption, in common with most of that generation, of a-moralism or agnosticism (we may refer again to *The Tragic Generation*), and of omnivorous reading in French literature. Of the poets that influenced the work to follow, we should notice above all François Villon;[2] for the characteristic blend of high lamentation for the passing of beauty, and for a brutality and violence that went to form, with much Elizabethan knowledge and precedent, his characteristic style. We have only to set against his own poem

> 'Seven dog-days we let pass
> Naming Queens in Glenmacnass,
> All the rare and royal names
> Wormy sheepskin yet retains:

[1] *Essays and Introductions* (1961), p. 299.
[2] We should see this, again, in the context of the 1890s; and in the light of R. L. Stevenson's essay, *A Lodging for the Night*.

> Etain, Helen, Maeve and Fand,
> Golden Deirdre's tender hand . . .'[1]

Villon's Ballade

> 'Dictes moy ou, n'en quel pays,
> Est Flora la belle Rommaine;
> Archipiada, ne Thais,
> Qui fut sa cousine germaine . . .'

to see the debt. There is, too, the concern, especially in *Riders to the Sea* and in *Deirdre*, with elemental sorrow.

> 'Et meure Paris ou Helaine,
> Quinconques meurt, meurt à douleur
> Telle qu'il perd vent et alaine;
> Son fiel se creve sur son cuer,
> Puis sue, Dieu scet quelle sueur!'

We may remember a passage from *Deirdre*, with its echo of burning Troy, the symbol that was so dear to Yeats:

> 'I see the flames of Emain starting upward in the dark night; and because of me there will be weazels and wild cats crying on a lonely wall where there were queens and armies and red gold, the way there will be a story told of a ruined city and a raving king and a woman will be young for ever.'

Much reading, then, in the Elizabethans and Jacobeans; Molière and La Pleiade and Villon; Petrarch and Cervantes; a knowledge of Irish, of Hebrew, and of music:

[1] *cf.* Nashe:

> 'Brightness falls from the air;
> Queens have died young and fair;
> Dust hath closed Helen's eye . . .'

we may add to these a detached yet compassionate view of humanity, and in particular of its failings, that seems so often to derive, historically, from an awareness of European literature. Above and behind it is the man himself; we may quote an eye-witness:

> 'La figure de Synge est typique: une tête longue, un peu carrée, aux traits tourmentés et, par moments, quasi douloureux, pas belle, mais singulièrement expressive. La moustache châtaine voile à demi les lèvres épaisses; une manière de gôitre enfle le côté droit du cou. Il se montre d'une courtoisie charmante, pleine d'aménité, de douceur, légèrement timide. L'intelligence est ouverte, accueillante.'[1]

And against this some sentences from Yeats:

> 'He had under modest and charming manners, in almost all things of life, a complete absorption in his own dream. I have never heard him praise any writer, living or dead, but some old French farce-writer. For him nothing existed but his thought. He claimed nothing for it aloud. He never said any of those self-confident things I am enraged into saying, but one knew that he valued nothing else. He was too confident for self-assertion. . . . One did not think of him as an egotist. He was too sympathetic in the ordinary affairs of life and too simple. In the arts he knew no language but his own.'[2]

It is this 'absorption in his own dream' that gives rise to his characteristic ambivalence of attitude. There is a profound love and understanding of nature and the Irish

[1] *cit.* Corkery: *Synge and Anglo Irish Literature*, p. 58.
[2] *Autobiographies* (1955), p. 512.

landscape, more apparent, perhaps, in the Essays; yet with it a dispassionate realization of its cruelty, loneliness, and the menaces of mountains and of sea. He is aware of the peasant with his qualities of stoic endurance, his sense of pagan sorrow; and of his brutality and violence in action or in thought.

> 'He told me that when he lived in some peasant's house, he tried to make those about him forget that he was there, and it is certain that he was silent in any crowded room. It is possible that low vitality helped him to be observant and contemplative. . . .'[1]

His peasants are perceived, maybe, at three levels; as inheritors of a dark and bitter pre-Christian Ireland; as living under the Christian sign in which the priest may be fallible but the naïve piety unquestioned; and the ranting, roaring, brutal world of the market-place and pub. And he sets against the 'stage Irishman' of fiction and of the music-halls, a grimmer but more 'joyful' reality; exaggerating at times what Bourgeois has called 'the coefficient of Hibernicism'.[2]

§iii THE PLAYBOY

The Playboy does not lend itself readily to classification; as we revolve it in our hands many facets take fire and light. One such suggests that it is sheer extravagant comedy, comedy with elements of strong farce in the 'resurrection' of Christy Mahon's father, and in the puncturing of the massive and heroic lie; yet which might have ended (for we are prepared from the first for a wedding)

---

[1] *Essays and Introductions* (1961), pp. 320-1.
[2] M. Bourgeois, *J.M.S. and the Irish Theatre*, p. 288.

with Pegeen winning her Playboy, and Old Mahon marrying the Widow Quin. From another point of view it may be said to be 'free' comedy, in which moral issues are transcended or ignored; and therefore the possibilities of misunderstanding are multiplied. Again, we may see it as Dionysiac comedy, in which the instincts have uninhibited play; in keeping with Synge's demand for what is 'superb and wild in reality'. So the Playboy himself becomes a country Don Juan, rejoicing in his new-found power to excite the admiration of women,[1] and the very language 'richly flavoured as a nut or an apple', surprises or shocks by its fine excess. Another facet is turned, and we see it as satire; on the proverbial willingness of the West to give shelter to the malefactor and murderer (this goes back to the Elizabethan wars of conquest, and beyond); and thus the Playboy himself may become a comic Oedipus, 'the man who killed his da'. There is satire, too, in the pursuit of man by woman, the comic reversal of the conventional view; and we may remember how both Shaw and Shakespeare turned that theme to account. Indeed, we may carry the mock-heroics still further, and see in Christy a sort of Odysseus (the wanderer, cast up and seeking refuge), his triumph in the village sports a parody of the Greek games; a tragi-comic theatre with the Widow Quin as Nausicaa, a chorus of girls, and the village pub for a palace.

But again we can see it, if we will, as tragedy. The Playboy finds his soul through a lie, the 'gallous story' of his parricide; under the stimulus of heady admiration from men and women he grows in stature and in poetry:

---

[1] We may remember Othello's reported wooing of Desdemona: 'Mark me with what violence she first loved the Moor but for bragging and telling her fantastical lies.'

because he is indeed of the company of poets, 'fine fiery fellows with great rages when their temper's roused'. Under the blow of his father's reappearance he staggers, weakens, and finally compromises, though with a new certainty of himself. In this tragedy it is the girl who suffers; Pegeen has found her man, made him, won him in the teeth of opposition from her own sex. The marriage has been blessed by her father who emerges as a 'round' character in one superb drunken speech; from that marriage would spring, no doubt, because of the heroic and virile virtues of Christy, a band of 'gallant little swearers by the name of God'. (We may recall, in terms not widely dissimilar, Edmund's defence of his bastardy in *King Lear*.) And at the end Pegeen's loss is absolute, beyond comfort, for she has lost both the illusion and the reality; her despairing cry has the very ring of tragedy:

'Oh, my grief, I've lost him surely. I've lost the only Playboy of the Western World.'

All these facets, then, may be seen as we revolve the play in our thoughts, or bring it to life on the stage; by production, indeed, we may shade or emphasize some of them, but never (because the play is strong and sinewy and wholly self-consistent) avoid the impression that it runs its course between antimonies. This Synge intended, and we may quote from his letter to the press after the storm of abuse which its production aroused:

'*The Playboy* is not a play with a "purpose" in the modern sense of the word,'

(he is thinking, perhaps, of Shaw, Brieux, and the popular misrepresentations of Ibsen as a didactic dramatist)

—'but, although parts of it are or are meant to be

extravagant comedy, still a great deal that is in it and a great deal more that is behind it is perfectly serious when looked at in a certain light. This is often the case, I think, with comedy, and no one is quite sure today whether Shylock or Alceste should be played seriously or not. There are, it might be hinted, several sides to *The Playboy*'.[1]

Now it is this 'liberty of interpretation', the sinister position of Synge as a member of the suspect Anglo-Irish Protestant 'Ascendancy', the varying capacities of the audience to react to the play as a whole, and a suspicious memory of Yeats' difficulties over *The Countess Cathleen* that gave rise to what is now known as 'The Playboy Controversy'.

§iv CONTROVERSY AND RIOTS

Synge's conflict with outraged Irish morality began as far back as 1903, when the portrait of Nora in *The Shadow in the Glen* was felt to be a slur on Irish womanhood. But the week that followed the first production of *The Playboy* on 26th January, 1907, was a continuous riot, with that hysteria which recalls the first production of Victor Hugo's *Hernani* (with its violation of the formal alexandrine) or the reception of Ibsen's *Ghosts* in London. We may quote from Lady Gregory:

'There was a battle of a week. Every night protestors with their trumpets came and raised a din. Every night the police carried some of them off to the police courts. Every afternoon the paper gave reports of the trial before a magistrate who had not heard or read the

[1] *cit.* Bourgeois, p. 208.

play and who insisted on being given details of its inci-
dents by the accused and by the police. . . . There was a
very large audience on the first night. . . . Synge was
there, but Mr Yeats was giving a lecture in Scotland.
The first act got its applause, and the second, though
one felt that the audience were a little puzzled, a little
shocked at the wild language. Near the end of the third
act there was some hissing. We had sent a telegram to
Mr Yeats after the end of the first act "Play great success"; but at the end we sent another—"Audience broke
up in disorder at the word shift".[1]

It is possible to deduce the main causes of offence,
however innocent these may seem to a modern audience.
In the first act the audience may well have been 'a little
puzzled' by the apparent glorification of parricide, or by
the 'heroic' aspects of murder; countless jests on the violence of the agrarian troubles, the Phoenix Park murders,
had left some consciences a little raw. And there was
warrant for it:

'An old man on the Aran Islands told me the very tale
on which The Playboy is founded, beginning with the
words: "If any gentleman has done a crime we'll hide
him. There was a gentleman that killed his father, and I
had him in my own house six months till he got away to
America".[2]

As for the 'wild language', Lady Gregory had indeed pro-
tested against its coarseness before the play was produced;
but Synge's purpose was to produce a kind of meta-

[1] cit. Ellis-Fermor, p. 50.
[2] Essays and Introductions (1961), p. 337-8. Synge's own version is
given in The Aran Islands.

physical shock, by a wild conjunction of opposites, to communicate what he understood by his 'reality and joy'. For the Dublin conscience there was, perhaps, more than a suspicion that the innocent and naïve blasphemies of the peasantry might acquire sinister implications from the pen of a Protestant:

'Is it killed your father?'
'With the help of God I did, surely, and that the Holy Immaculate Mother may intercede for his soul.'[1]

But behind and above all this there is the case of the offensive line which seems to have triggered off the riot:

'. . . a drift of chosen females, standing in their shifts itself, maybe, from this place to the Eastern world.'

The rancour of the mob centred on the fatal *shift*; in an access of outraged modesty, Victorian in character, but connected somehow with the idea that the very word was insulting to the womanhood of Ireland: whose chastity, purity, even sainthood had become a national myth, even as the saintliness of the Island as a whole. The word, indeed, was far more highly charged than the famous 'Not bloody likely!' of Shaw's *Pygmalion*, a phrase which our study of semantics has now rendered trite. And it seems probable that the audience, in their concentration, missed the more subtle point of the phrase; for the picture of the Mayo maidens perceived as a throng of Eastern houris is rendered yet more fantastic in that the term *drift*

---

[1] Bourgeois (*op. cit.*) considers that this speech is beyond probability: a peasant would say one or the other, but not both. I disagree; the two clauses in the second sentence are no more than pious ejaculations, which have even assumed the nature of clichés, and might achieve, though infrequently, such a conjunction.

is normally applied to a drove of heifers. There was, of course, the additional offence: an Irish woman would never admire a murderer, or even sleep, unchaperoned, under the same roof with a man.

The attack on *The Playboy* was not confined to Dublin; and we may again quote Yeats:

'Picturesque, poetical, fantastical, a masterpiece of style and of music, the supreme work of our dialect theatre, his *Playboy* roused the populace to fury. We played it under police protection, seventy police in the theatre the last night, and five hundred, some newspaper said, keeping order in the streets outside. It is never played before any Irish audience for the first time without something or other being flung at the players. In New York a currant cake and a watch were flung, the owner of the watch claiming it at the stage-door afterwards. The Dublin audience has, however, long since accepted the play.'[1]

And again:

'The Irish nationalists in America mobilized every force they could touch to boycott the (Abbey) plays throughout the Eastern States. The fight took much the same form everywhere, though it was fiercer in some towns than in others. It started in a prejudice, not the less violent for its ignorance and generally among members of the Gaelic League, against the picture of Irish life and morals which the plays of the new school were said to give. The general prejudice was entangled with and sometimes manipulated by political prejudices of a far-reaching and almost infinitely complex kind. And

[1] *Autobiographies* (1955), p. 570. (This was written in 1925.)

mingled again with both was the religious prejudice of some sections at least of the Church.'[1]

§ V IRONY

Now of all the possible sources of misunderstanding in a play the most fecund is the dramatist's use of irony: whether of word, situation, or idea; and it is possible to argue that the more subtle and dispassionate the use of this, the less likely he is to achieve full and immediate communication of it in the theatre. Further, the perception of irony will vary with the type of audience and with its age: full enlightenment demands at least a measure of values, traditions, background and a sense both of humour or wit that are held in common between the writer and his public.

Synge's attitude to Ireland and to the Irish peasantry was highly ambivalent: we may think of broadly similar positions taken up, at different times, by Swift, Shaw, Yeats.[2] Love and understanding are not inseparable from a detached mockery. But the union of these may be so subtle, so fluctuating, and yet so integral to the whole system of values in the play, that we may examine briefly some of the instances.

This irony is founded most often on incongruity, in the perception of polar opposites: and it is precisely when one of the poles between which the irony is discharged is felt to be unacceptable that misunderstanding is most apt to arise. If we consider the following:

. . . 'or Marcus Quin, God rest him, got six months for maiming ewes—'

[1] Ellis-Fermor, *op. cit.*, p. 54.
[2] 'I once said to John Synge, "Do you write out of love or hate of Ireland?" and he replied, "I have often asked myself that question."' Yeats, *Letters*, ed. Wade, p. 618.

('God rest him' being the normal pious expletive concerning anyone who is dead, but here a little incongruous with his crime)

—'and he a great warrant to tell stories of holy Ireland—'

where the second clause links 'holy Ireland' with 'God rest him', and both combine ironically with the 'six months for maiming ewes'. But against this triangle there are two background references: the Moonlighters and the Agrarian Troubles generally, and the endless references to Holy Ireland, The Isle of Saints, and so forth. It is the kind of reference embodied in Yeats' poem:

'Beautiful lofty things: O'Leary's noble head;
My father upon the Abbey stage, before him a raging crowd:
"This Land of Saints", and then as the applause died out,
"Of plaster Saints"; his beautiful mischievous head thrown back.'

Something of the same metaphysical perception is in Shawn's agonized cry:

'Oh, Father Reilly, and the saints of God, where will I hide myself today?'

or the point of Sara's speech as she tries on the boots:

'There's a pair do fit me well, and I'll be keeping them for walking to the priest, when you'd be ashamed this place, going up winter and summer with nothing worth while to confess at all.'[1]

---

[1] Yeats told a story of a priest who had just confessed a convent of nuns. 'It was like being nibbled to death by ducks.'

—set against a fragment of dialogue from *The Tinker's Wedding*:

> *Priest*: 'What would you do if it was the like of myself you were, saying Mass with your mouth dry, and running east and west for a sick call maybe, and hearing the rural people again and they saying their sins?'

> *Mary* (with compassion): 'It's destroyed you must be hearing the sins of the rural people on a fine spring.'

Let us be frank about it: Synge's satire is constantly directed, with greater or less point, against certain aspects of Roman Catholicism, as he saw it in the West of Ireland. That in itself was sufficient cause of offence: and the more delicate the irony the more profound the sense of injury. But there is, here and particularly in *The Well of the Saints*, the intricate question of the relation of the dream-world to the reality, of the lie to the fact, of the narrated or epically-conceived murder to a real one; of the validity of the poet's vision, and even his rights, when confronted with the world. Here, in play after play, is the source of Synge's irony: subtle, shifting, counterpointed. It may range from this:

> *Nora*: 'Didn't the young priest say the Almighty God won't leave her destitute with no son living?'

> *Maurya*: 'It's little the like of *him* knows of the sea . . .'

to the farcical scene in which the priest is put in a sack by the tinkers, and has his revenge (for he has promised not to 'have the law of them') by pronouncing a Latin malediction.

§vi THE LANGUAGE

Much has been written of Synge's language; and the adverse criticisms range from St John Ervine's indictment of him as a 'faker of peasant speech' to T. S. Eliot's more reasonable and more reasoned view:

> 'The plays of John Millington Synge form rather a special case, because they are based upon the idiom of a rural people whose speech is naturally poetic, both in imagery and in rhythm. I believe that he even incorporated phrases which he had heard from these country people of Ireland' (we may admire this phrasing). 'The language of Synge is not available except for the plays set among that same people. . . . But in order to be poetic in prose, a dramatist has to be so consistently poetic that his scope is very limited. Synge wrote plays about characters whose originals in life talked poetically, so that he could make them talk poetry and remain real people.'[1]

Let us admit at the outset the disadvantages and limitations of this poetic diction. It is fatally easy to write—in one kind. It lends itself readily both to parody and to imitation at the hands of inferior dramatists. It degenerates very easily into a stereotyped and cliché-ridden jargon. In *The Playboy* it gives at times the impression of a certain congestion. It does not, as Mr Eliot hints, lend itself to 'low-tension' or 'bridging' passages of the narrative kind. Its faults appear all too plainly when it is used for translation, as in Synge's own versions of Petrarch; and we may consider the relative failure of this in comparison with the fresh vividness of the Italian:

[1] T. S. Eliot, *Poetry and Drama*, pp. 19-20.

The fine time of the year increases Petrarch's sorrow.

The south wind is coming back, bringing the
fine season, and the flowers, and the grass,
her sweet family, along with her. The swallow
and the nightingale are making a stir, and the
spring is turning white and red in every place.

There is a cheerful look on the meadows, and peace
in the sky, and the sun is well pleased,
I'm thinking, looking downward, and the air
and the waters and the earth herself are full
of love, and every beast is turning back looking
for its mate.

And what is coming to me is great sighing and
trouble, which herself is drawing out of my
deep heart, herself that has taken the key
of it up to Heaven.

And it is this way I am, that the singing birds
and the flowers of the earth, and the sweet
ladies, with their grace and comeliness, are the
like of a desert to me, and wild beasts astray
in it.

We are made uneasy by the excessive use of present par-
ticiples; the interjection *I'm thinking*; the inversion of
And what is coming to me is; the Irishism of *herself is
dreaming*; the slightly sentimental flavour of the third
verse. But it is best to return to Synge's own intention.

'In a good play every speech should be as fully
flavoured as a nut or an apple. . . . In Ireland, for a few
years more, we have a popular imagination that is fiery,
and magnificent, and tender. . . .'

'. . . in countries where the imagination of the people, and the language they use is rich and living, it is possible for a writer to be rich and copious in his words, and at the same time to give the reality, which is the root of all poetry, in a comprehensive and natural form.'

Now I see no reason to doubt Synge's oft-quoted story of listening to the conversation in the farmhouse kitchen in Wicklow, his ear to the chinks in the floor of the room above it. Neither do I see the need for it. A man who had moved about the countryside, watching birds and landscape, or fishing in mountain tarns, whose family owned property in the West, would know, instinctively, much that was in 'the book of the people'. Indeed I believe that the kitchen legend has done much harm, as suggesting that the speech of Synge's character is naturalistic to an extent that he never intended, and that no dramatic speech can ever be. Yet there is truth in the accusation of undue artificiality, and it is well to examine it.

A listener who is known and trusted,[1] in converse with the peasantry of those times, would have heard, perhaps once or twice in an hour, perhaps no more than once in a week, a single memorable phrase, 'as fully flavoured as a nut or an apple', that might be treasured and re-minted in a poem or a play. But they were few; Synge worked by a process of accumulation, intensification, compression. Of this Bickley[2] quotes an example. The original was:

'Listen to what I'm telling you: a man who is not married is no better than an old jackass. He goes into his sister's house, and into his brother's house; he eats

---

[1] for the casual visitor will, in tourist centres, be met with 'manufactured' idiom.

[2] F. L. Bickley, *J.M.S.* The original passage is in *The Aran Islands*.

a bit in this place and a bit in another place, but he has no home for himself, like an old jackass straying upon the rocks.'

Now the centre of the image is the 'unmarried man', the 'old jackass' resemblance; the rocks may be those of the sea-shore,[1] but more likely the stony outcrop of the Burren country and Aran, with small pockets of grass growing in the crevices; the whole suggests the wandering, half-starved, aimless life. Synge compresses it all, and holds back the key-words for the cadence and for the climax:

'What's a single man, I ask you, eating a bit in one house and drinking a sup in another, and he with no place of his own, like an old braying jackass strayed upon the rocks?'

We may well feel uneasy at the jingle of *braying* and *strayed*, through Synge's attempt to achieve 'richness'; but the whole has been re-set to give the characteristic rhythm. This rhythm is central to Synge's art; and is so highly-wrought that the accusation of 'literariness' is not without justification. We can examine briefly some of its characteristics.

Of these the most important is the cadence,[2] the pattern of weak and strong accents at the end of a phrase, and giving the effect, perhaps, of the resolution of chords in music. The cadence is denoted by counting the stresses *backward* from the last syllables; it is of two main types, the Latin (familiar through the rhythm of the Mass passing over in translation into the Liturgy) which has the strong stress on the penultimate syllable, and the native

[1] where cattle often graze, rather precariously.
[2] See, *e.g.*, N. R. Tempest, *The Rhythm of English Prose*, Ch. III.

or English cadence which has the stress on the final syllable. We may perceive the 'patterns' readily; they are sometimes reinforced by alliteration:

... with a *n*osegay in her golde*n* shawl	(6 : 3 : 1)
... I'm master of all *f*ights *f*rom now	(6 : 3 : 1)
... that young gaffer who'd cap*s*ize the star*s*	(6 : 3 : 1)

and the 'extension' of this

... paving the laneway to your door	(7 : 4 : 1)

Sometimes whole lines of blank verse may be noted in the rhythmic pattern.

This strong rhythm may become monotonous in reading: on the stage (and Synge took much trouble with his actors' speech) it is redeemed by the variety of tone, pitch and voice-cadence, which together give variety, emphasis and momentum. In amateur productions it is best to let the prose speak for itself, rather than attempt to superimpose upon it any kind of so-called 'Irish brogue'. The speech of the Western peasant is subtle in its tones, and not easily imitated; but if the prose is understood while it is spoken it will be found to convey in tone and pitch at least something of its own subtlety and its variety of speed.

'Synge found the check that suited his temperament in an elaboration of the dialects of Kerry and Aran. The cadence is long and meditative, as befits the thought of men who are much alone, and who when they meet in one another's houses—as their way is at the day's end—listen patiently, each man speaking in turn and for some little time, and taking pleasure in the vaguer meaning of the words and in their sound.'[1]

[1] *Essays and Introductions* (1961), p. 334.

On the matter of the structure of this prose we cannot do better than quote Bourgeois:

'The student who knows Gaelic still thinks in Gaelic as he reads or hears Synge's plays. This applies not only to the phraseology used by his characters, but to the syntax of their sentences. An aorist like "He is after doing", or co-ordination used instead of subordination in the Irishism "And he going to the fair" . . . are pure Gaelic constructions. Ancillary clauses, enallages, inversions and hyperbata of all kinds are unusually plentiful. . . .'[1]

The structure is not 'Elizabethan' Anglo-Irish, for that it is more apparent in the East and South-East, where the influence of Tudor invasions yet remains in the speech; though it is well to remember such a construction as

'For I determined not to know anything among you, save Jesus Christ, and him crucified.'[2]

is solely 'Irish'. And indeed Synge borrows much from the Bible and from the Psalms—sources that no Catholic peasantry would use—as well as from the Elizabethans and the Gaelic.

But above all it is the intentional violence, richness and exaggeration of imagery that has given rise to most of the attacks on Synge. Behind 'the nut and the apple' there is, perhaps, Spenser:

'Euen so doe those rough and harsh termes enlumine and make more clearly to appeare the brightnesse of braue and glorious wordes.'[3]

[1] *op. cit.* p. 226.
[2] I *Cor.* II.2.
[3] Preface to *S.K.*

It is difficult to deny that Synge does at times strain after his rhetorical effects: as in

> ... 'till you'd find a radiant lady with droves of bullocks on the plains of Meath, and herself bedizened in the diamond jewelleries of Pharoh's ma.'

or the even more famous

> ... 'do be straining the bars of Paradise to lay eyes on the Lady Helen of Troy, and she abroad, pacing back and forward, with a nosegay in her golden shawl.'

But there are not many of these strokes of *opus Alexandrinum*. We may accept

> 'that young gaffer who'd capsize the stars'

remembering Marlow and Roy Campbell,[1] or

> 'Oh, aren't you a heathen daughter to go shaking the fat of my heart, and I swamped and drownded with the weight of drink?'

against

> 'Thou whoreson little tidy Bartholomew boar-pig, when wilt thou leave fighting o'days, and foining o' nights, and begin to patch up thine old body for heaven?'[2]

or that optative (common cliché in prayer or curse)

> ... 'and that the Lord God would send a high wave to wash him from the world.'[3]

---

[1] *e.g. The Flaming Terrapin*, II.
[2] II *Henry IV*, II.4.235.
[3] A memory of the *Hippolytus?*

There are indeed instances where 'the wheels take fire from the mere rapidity of their motion'; and here again we may quote Yeats:

> 'He made his own selection of word and phrase, choosing what would express his own personality. . . .'[1] Perhaps no Irish countryman had ever that exact rhythm in his voice, but certainly if Mr Synge had been born a countryman, he would have spoken like that. . . .'[2]

Against these we may set the memorable things, in all their variety, that are concerned organically to convey, not only shades of character, but a wide variety of lyric and elegiac moods.

§vii THE BACKGROUND OF THE PLAY

The scene of *The Playboy* could be fixed with some accuracy by a detective-minded geographer: it is obviously in North-West Mayo, within sight of the sea and of that dominant mountain, Nephin, a great landmark of those parts; it is not far from Belmullet and Castlebar. But the locale is of no great consequence; it is the general setting that matters. The remote public house is also a sort of general store; the widely-scattered cabins; the vistas of mountain, sea and bog made translucent and melancholy in the rain-washed air; the imagination of its people focused on Dante's three subjects, love and war and death. In the pub itself we are aware, as in Jack Yeats' drawings, of the smell of porter, and strong plug tobacco, and horses, and rough wet Mayo frieze. But above all it is a world of contradictions, and ambivalences: of kind-

[1] *Essays and Introductions* (1961), p. 299.
[2] *Ibid*, p. 300.

ness and cruelty; of a great and untidy[1] preoccupation
with death; of violent contrasts between the seasons; of a
simple yet sometimes strangely contradictory religious
faith. Above all it is a world of loneliness and bitter toil
for the women; let Nora speak from *The Shadow of the
Glen*:

> —'for what good is a bit of a farm with cows on it, and
> sheep on the back hills, when you do be sitting looking
> out from a door the like of that door, and seeing nothing
> but the mists rolling down the bog, and the mists again
> and they rolling up the bog, and hearing nothing but the
> wind crying out in the bits of broken trees were left
> from the great storm, and the streams roaring with the
> rain.'

It is a world in which women age prematurely, worn
by often excessive child-bearing and toil in the cabin and
the muddy farmsteads; feeding animals and fowls; the
work in the fields or on the strands:

> 'You've plucked a curlew, drawn a hen,
> Washed the shirts of seven men,
> You've stuffed my pillow, stretched the sheet,
> And filled the pan to wash your feet . . .'

Girlhood and courtship are made frustrating and difficult, not merely by the priests but by 'a fear of the passions that is older than Christianity'. Marriage, usually
arranged, is often to an older man, so that we have the
situation of *The Shadow of the Glen*; the alternative—see

[1] 'For death should be a queer untidy thing, though it's a queen
that dies.' (*Deirdre*). See, too, the description of a churchyard by
T. H. White; *The Godstone and the Blackymor*; and Synge's
own poem, *In Kerry*.

again *The Vanishing Irish*—is migration to the infinitely greater freedom, and perhaps fulfilment, of England. And in Synge's world we are conscious, as it were, of an outer ring of a dominating alien land; the peelers, the 'loosèd khaki' soldiers, the hanging judges and venal juries waiting for the law-breaker in the assize towns; so that the shelter of a murderer, perhaps even the knocking out of a policeman's eye or the maiming of a landlord's cattle, is praiseworthy and glorious up to the exact point where one becomes likely to be involved with the law. For this explains the attempt to rope the Playboy after he has committed his supposed second murder; not only is the deed a dirty one instead of 'a gallous story', but there are now too many witnesses. Death and life; with a strange delight in imagined or anticipated violence, the desired ends of a great death and a clean, or a costly funeral: defiance and a fatalism that is half-pagan, half-Christian:

'No one at all can be living for ever, and we must be satisfied.'

Yet, whatever the resignation, these people drink perpetually of sorrow's springs, and the wild lament for the dead is never far away.

§viii THE SOLITARY MAN

The work of Synge is slight in bulk, but it is a unity; the plays, prose and verse certifying and confirming each other as to tone, attitude, and idiom, so that all should be read. *In Wicklow and West Kerry* and *The Aran Islands* can show us how the stone lay in his quarry; the poems show his roots in Villon, and his concern with that timber that has its roots among the clay and the worms; the translations from Petrarch and Villon show his use of the new language and rhythms; and their very strict limitations for that purpose. Above all, the remaining plays must be read in relation to *The Playboy*. *The Shadow of the Glen* fills in something of the background of woman's loneliness and defeat, as well as the mystery of the hills and the lament for the passing of youth; with life oscillating between the poetry of the Tramp and the brutal and sordid realities of living. *The Tinker's Wedding* gives us Synge's insight into the minds of woman and of priest, the roaring violence of farce. *The Well of the Saints* brings up in another form a theme of *The Playboy*; do we live by the dream or by the fact, and is not man's capacity for self-delusion a protection for the little happiness he may win? *Riders to the Sea* gives us tragedy in its most profound and inexorable simplicity; less violent, more lyric than the rest in language, more elegiac in its tone, achieving depth by common yet complex symbols, against the forces of time and the sea. And *Deirdre* itself lives in another kind; heroic tragedy brought nearer and intensified by the language that by now is so familiar; and living in a few great lyric phrases:

'It is not a small thing to be rid of grey hairs,
and the loosening of the teeth.'

§ix

But Synge was a solitary man, and no one could follow him. Peasant plays indeed followed him in plenty, so that 'P.Q.' (peasant quality) is now a term of dramatic classification and sometimes of contempt. The vein of ore which he worked was small and soon exhausted; his

manner, his diction, even the general types of his characters, are fatally easy to imitate, and could and did degener-
ate into the mannered diction called Kiltartanese, from
the village near Lady Gregory's Coole Park. For Yeats
could only (and then with Lady Gregory's help) imitate
Synge's language, and had none of Synge's insight into
character: Lady Gregory herself could achieve a comedy
as refined as her gay and gracious nature, and a tragedy,
pathetic or patriotic, fitted to her vision and gifts. It was
left for Sean O'Casey to transplant tragedy to the Dublin
slums, and to forge a new speech for it, being finely
touched with the great issues of two wars. None could
achieve, or indeed wished to achieve, these ambivalent
complexities of mood and intention, this fierce ironic joy
in the brutal or the glorious phrase, this combination of
passionate insight into simplicity with the grim detach-
ment of the 'disinterested' artist. Yet again, he is perhaps
a preacher, a preacher who is agnostic or a-moral, whose
text is the living world. It is a world whose tragedy is
always close, but where that tragedy may be dissolved
or reinforced by laughter, the imagination nourished by
its humour; where extremities meet and clash to illumine,
intermittently, the human situation, and its 'complexities
of mire and blood'.

Persons in the play

CHRISTOPHER MAHON

OLD MAHON, his father, a squatter

MICHAEL JAMES FLAHERTY (called MICHAEL JAMES), a publican

MARGARET FLAHERTY (called PEGEEN MIKE), his daughter

WIDOW QUIN, a woman of about thirty

SHAWN KEOGH, her cousin, a young farmer

PHILLY CULLEN and JIMMY FARRELL, small farmers

SARA TANSEY, SUSAN BRADY and HONOR BLAKE, village girls

A BELLMAN

SOME PEASANTS

The action takes place near a village, on a wild coast of Mayo. The first Act passes on an evening of autumn, the other two Acts on the following day

Preface

In writing 'The Playboy of the Western World', as in my other plays, I have used one or two words only that I have not heard among the country people of Ireland, or spoken in my own nursery before I could read the newspapers. A certain number of the phrases I employ I have heard also from herds and fishermen along the coast from Kerry to Mayo or from beggar-women and ballad-singers nearer Dublin; and I am glad to acknowledge how much I owe to the folk-imagination of these fine people. Anyone who has lived in real intimacy with the Irish peasantry will know that the wildest sayings and ideas in this play are tame indeed, compared with the fancies one may hear in any little hillside cabin in Geesala, or Carraroe, or Dingle Bay. All art is a collaboration; and there is little doubt that in the happy ages of literature, striking and beautiful phrases were as ready to the story-teller's or the playwright's hand, as the rich cloaks and dresses of his time. It is probable that when the Elizabethan dramatist took his ink-horn and sat down to his work he used many phrases that he had just heard, as he sat at dinner, from his mother or his children. In Ireland, those of us who know the people have the same privilege. When I was writing *The Shadow of the Glen*, some years ago, I got more aid than any learning could have given me from a chink in the floor of the old Wicklow house where I was staying, that let me hear what was being said by the servant girls in the kitchen. This matter, I think, is of importance, for in countries where the imagination of the people, and the language they use, is rich and living, it is possible for a writer to be rich and copious in his words, and at the same time to give the reality, which is the root of all poetry, in a comprehensive and natural form. In the modern literature of towns, however, richness is found only in sonnets, or prose poems, or in one or two elaborate books that are far away from the profound and common interests of life. One has, on one side, Mallarmé and Huysmans producing this literature; and on the other, Ibsen and Zola dealing with the reality of life in joyless and pallid works. On the stage one must have reality, and one must have joy; and that is why the intellectual modern drama has failed, and people have grown sick of the false joy of the musical comedy, that has been given them in place of the rich joy found only in what is superb and wild in reality. In a good play every speech should be as fully flavoured as a nut or apple, and such speeches cannot be written by any one who works among people who have shut their lips on poetry. In Ireland, for a few years more, we have a popular imagination that is fiery, and magnificent, and tender; so that those of us who wish to write start with a chance that is not given to writers in places where the springtime of the local life has been forgotten, and the harvest is a memory only, and the straw has been turned into bricks.

J.M.S.

21st January, 1907.

The Playboy of the Western World

ACT I

*Country public house or shebeen, very rough and untidy.
There is a sort of counter on the right with shelves, holding many bottles and jugs, just seen above it. Empty barrels stand near the counter. At back, a little to left of
counter, there is a door into the open air, then, more to the
left, there is a settle with shelves above it, with more jugs,
and a table beneath a window. At the left there is a large
open fireplace, with turf fire, and a small door into inner
room. Pegeen, a wild-looking but fine girl, of about
twenty, is writing at table. She is dressed in the usual
peasant dress.*

PEGEEN [*Slowly as she writes*] Six yards of stuff for to
make a yellow gown. A pair of lace boots with lengthy
heels on them and brassy eyes. A hat is suited for a
wedding day. A fine-tooth comb. To be sent with
three barrels of porter in Jimmy Farrell's creel cart on
the evening of the coming Fair to Mister Michael James
Flaherty. With the best compliments of this season.
Margaret Flaherty.

SHAWN KEOGH [*A fat and fair young man comes in as she
signs, looks around awkwardly, when he sees she is
alone*] Where's himself?

*supposed to
be a wedding*

PEGEEN [*Without looking at him*] He's coming. [*She directs letter*] To Mister Sheamus Mulroy, Wine and Spirit Dealer, Castlebar.

SHAWN [*Uneasily*] I didn't see him on the road.

PEGEEN How would you see him [*licks stamp and puts it on letter*] and it dark night this half-hour gone by?

SHAWN [*Turning towards door again*] I stood a while outside wondering would I have a right to pass on or to walk in and see you, Pegeen Mike [*comes to fire*], and I could hear the cows breathing and sighing in the stillness of the air, and not a step moving any place from this gate to the bridge.

PEGEEN [*Putting letter in envelope*] It's above at the cross-roads he is, meeting Philly Cullen and a couple more are going along with him to Kate Cassidy's wake.

SHAWN [*Looking at her blankly*] And he's going that length in the dark night.

PEGEEN [*Impatiently*] He is surely, and leaving me lonesome on the scruff of the hill. [*She gets up and puts envelope on dresser, then winds clock*] Isn't it long the nights are now, Shawn Keogh, to be leaving a poor girl with her own self counting the hours to the dawn of day?

SHAWN [*With awkward humour*] If it is, when we're wedded in a short while you'll have no call to complain, for I've little will to be walking off to wakes or weddings in the darkness of the night.

PEGEEN [*With rather scornful good humour*] You're making mighty certain, Shaneen, that I'll wed you now.

SHAWN Aren't we after making a good bargain, the way we're only waiting these days on Father Reilly's dispensation from the bishops, or the Court of Rome.

PEGEEN [*Looking at him teasingly, washing up at dresser*]

42

It's a wonder, Shaneen, the Holy Father'd be taking notice of the likes of you; for if I was him I wouldn't bother with this place where you'll meet none but Red Linahan, has a squint in his eye, and Patcheen is lame in his heel, or the mad Mulrannies were driven from California and they lost in their wits. We're a queer lot these times to go troubling the Holy Father on his sacred seat.

SHAWN [*Scandalized*] If we are, we're as good this place as another, maybe, and as good these times as we were for ever.

[handwritten margin note: nothing wrong. according to shawn]

PEGEEN [*With scorn*] As good it is? Where now will you meet the like of Daneen Sullivan knocked the eye from a peeler; or Marcus Quin, God rest him, got six months for maiming ewes, and he a great warrant to tell stories of holy Ireland till he'd have the old women shedding down tears about their feet. Where will you find the like of them, I'm saying?

[handwritten margin note: her brand of excitement]

SHAWN [*Timidly*] If you don't, it's a good job, maybe; for [*with peculiar emphasis on the words*] Father Reilly has small conceit to have that kind walking around and talking to the girls.

PEGEEN [*Impatiently throwing water from basin out of the door*] Stop tormenting me with Father Reilly [*imitating his voice*] when I'm asking only what way I'll pass these twelve hours of dark, and not take my death with the fear. [*Looking out of door*]

SHAWN [*Timidly*] Would I fetch you the Widow Quin, maybe?

PEGEEN Is it the like of that murderer? You'll not, surely.

SHAWN [*Going to her, soothingly*] Then I'm thinking himself will stop along with you when he sees you taking on; for it'll be a long night-time with great

43

darkness, and I'm after feeling a kind of fellow above in the furzy ditch, groaning wicked like a maddening dog, the way it's good cause you have, maybe, to be fearing now.

PEGEEN [*Turning on him sharply*] What's that? Is it a man you seen?

SHAWN [*Retreating*] I couldn't see him at all; but I heard him groaning out, and breaking his heart. It should have been a young man from his words speaking.

PEGEEN [*Going after him*] And you never went near to see was he hurted or what ailed him at all?

SHAWN I did not, Pegeen Mike. It was a dark, lonesome place to be hearing the like of him.

PEGEEN Well, you're a daring fellow, and if they find his corpse stretched above in the dews of dawn, what'll you say then to the peelers, or the Justice of the Peace?

SHAWN [*Thunderstruck*] I wasn't thinking of that. For the love of God, Pegeen Mike, don't let on I was speaking of him. Don't tell your father and the men is coming above; for if they heard that story they'd have great blabbing this night at the wake.

PEGEEN I'll maybe tell them, and I'll maybe not.

SHAWN They are coming at the door. Will you whisht, I'm saying?

PEGEEN Whisht yourself.

[*She goes behind counter. Michael James, fat, jovial publican, comes in followed by Philly Cullen, who is thin and mistrusting, and Jimmy Farrell, who is fat and amorous, about forty-five*]

MEN [*Together*] God bless you! The blessing of God on this place!

PEGEEN God bless you kindly.

MICHAEL [*To men, who go to the counter*] Sit down now,

44

and take your rest. [*Crosses to Shawn at the fire*] And how is it you are, Shawn Keogh? Are you coming over the sands to Kate Cassidy's wake?

SHAWN I am not, Michael James. I'm going home the short cut to my bed.

PEGEEN [*Speaking across the counter*] He's right, too, and have you no shame, Michael James, to be quitting off for the whole night, and leaving myself lonesome in the shop?

MICHAEL [*Good-humouredly*] Isn't it the same whether I go for the whole night or a part only? and I'm thinking it's a queer daughter you are if you'd have me crossing backward through the Stooks of the Dead Women, with a drop taken.

PEGEEN If I am a queer daughter, it's a queer father'd be leaving me lonesome these twelve hours of dark, and I piling the turf with the dogs barking, and the calves mooing, and my own teeth rattling with the fear.

JIMMY [*Flatteringly*] What is there to hurt you, and you a fine, hardy girl would knock the heads of any two men in the place?

PEGEEN [*Working herself up*] Isn't there the harvest boys with their tongues red for drink, and the ten tinkers is camped in the east glen, and the thousand militia—bad cess to them!—walking idle through the land. There's lots surely to hurt me, and I won't stop alone in it, let himself do what he will.

[handwritten marginal note:] utterly irresistable — ask her.

MICHAEL If you're that afeard, let Shawn Keogh stop along with you. It's the will of God, I'm thinking, himself should be seeing to you now. [*They all turn on Shawn*]

SHAWN [*In horrified confusion*] I would and welcome, Michael James, but I'm afeard of Father Reilly; and what at all would the Holy Father and the Cardinals of Rome be saying if they heard I did the like of that?

MICHAEL [*With contempt*] God help you! Can't you sit in by the hearth with the light lit and herself beyond in the room? You'll do that surely, for I've heard tell there's a queer fellow above, going mad or getting his death, maybe, in the gripe of the ditch, so she'd be safer this night with a person here.

SHAWN [*With plaintive despair*] I'm afeard of Father Reilly, I'm saying. Let you not be tempting me, and we near married itself.

PHILLY [*With cold contempt*] Lock him in the west room. He'll stay then and have no sin to be telling to the priest.

MICHAEL [*To Shawn, getting between him and the door*] Go up, now.

SHAWN [*At the top of his voice*] Don't stop me, Michael James. Let me out of the door, I'm saying, for the love of the Almighty God. Let me out. [*Trying to dodge past him*] Let me out of it, and may God grant you His indulgence in the hour of need.

MICHAEL [*Loudly*] Stop your noising, and sit down by the hearth. [*Gives him a push and goes to counter laughing*]

SHAWN [*Turning back, wringing his hands*] Oh, Father Reilly, and the saints of God, where will I hide myself today? Oh, St Joseph and St Patrick and St Brigid and St James, have mercy on me now!

[*Shawn turns round, sees door clear, and makes a rush for it*]

MICHAEL [*Catching him by the coat-tail*] You'd be going, is it?

SHAWN [*Screaming*] Leave me go, Michael James, leave

46

me go, you old Pagan, leave me go, or I'll get the curse
of the priests on you, and of the scarlet-coated bishops
of the Courts of Rome.

[*With a sudden movement he pulls himself out of his
coat, and disappears out of the door, leaving his
coat in Michael's hands*]

MICHAEL [*Turning round, and holding up coat*] Well,
there's the coat of a Christian man. Oh, there's sainted
glory this day in the lonesome west; and by the will of
God I've got you a decent man, Pegeen, you'll have no
call to be spying after if you've a score of young girls,
maybe, weeding in your fields.

PEGEEN [*Taking up the defence of her property*] What
right have you to be making game of a poor fellow for
minding the priest, when it's your own the fault is, not
paying a penny pot-boy to stand along with me and
give me courage in the doing of my work.

[*She snaps the coat away from him, and goes behind
counter with it*]

MICHAEL [*Taken aback*] Where would I get a pot-boy?
Would you have me send the bell-man screaming in
the streets of Castlebar?

SHAWN [*Opening the door a chink and putting in his
head, in a small voice*] Michael James!

MICHAEL [*Imitating him*] What ails you?

SHAWN The queer dying fellow's beyond looking over
the ditch. He's come up, I'm thinking, stealing your
hens. [*Looks over his shoulder*] God help me, he's
following me now [*he runs into room*], and if he's
heard what I said, he'll be having my life, and I going
home lonesome in the darkness of the night.

[*For a perceptible moment they watch the door with
curiosity. Someone coughs outside. Then Christy*]

47

*Mahon, a slight young man, comes in very tired
and frightened and dirty*]

CHRISTY [*In a small voice*] God save all here!

MEN God save you kindly!

CHRISTY [*Going to the counter*] I'd trouble you for a glass
of porter, woman of the house. [*He puts down coin*]

PEGEEN [*Serving him*] You're one of the tinkers, young
fellow, is beyond camped in the glen?

CHRISTY I am not; but I'm destroyed walking.

MICHAEL [*Patronizingly*] Let you come up then to the
fire. You're looking famished with the cold.

CHRISTY God reward you. [*He takes up his glass and goes
a little way across to the left, then stops and looks
about him*] Is it often the polis do be coming into this
place, master of the house?

MICHAEL If you'd come in better hours, you'd have seen
'Licensed for the Sale of Beer and Spirits, to be Con-
sumed on the Premises', written in white letters above
the door, and what would the polis want spying on me,
and not a decent house within four miles, the way every
living Christian is a bona fide, saving one widow alone?

CHRISTY [*With relief*] It's a safe house, so.

[*He goes over to the fire, sighing and moaning. Then
he sits down, putting his glass beside him, and
begins gnawing a turnip, too miserable to feel
the others staring at him with curiosity*]

MICHAEL [*Going after him*] Is it yourself is fearing the
polis? You're wanting, maybe?

CHRISTY There's many wanting. *mystery*

MICHAEL Many, surely, with the broken harvest and the
ended wars. [*He picks up some stockings, etc., that are
near the fire, and carries them away furtively*] It
should be larceny, I'm thinking?

48

CHRISTY [*Dolefully*] I had it in my mind it was a different word and a bigger.

PEGEEN There's a queer lad. Were you never slapped in school, young fellow, that you don't know the name of your deed?

CHRISTY [*Bashfully*] I'm slow at learning, a middling scholar only.

MICHAEL If you're a dunce itself, you'd have a right to know that larceny's robbing and stealing. Is it for the like of that you're wanting?

CHRISTY [*With a flash of family pride*] And I the son of a strong farmer [*with a sudden qualm*], God rest his soul, could have bought up the whole of your old house a while since, from the butt of his tail-pocket, and not have missed the weight of it gone.

MICHAEL [*Impressed*] If it's not stealing, it's maybe something big.

CHRISTY [*Flattered*] Aye; it's maybe something big.

JIMMY He's a wicked-looking young fellow. Maybe he followed after a young woman on a lonesome night.

CHRISTY [*Shocked*] Oh, the saints forbid, mister; I was all times a decent lad.

PHILLY [*Turning on Jimmy*] You're a silly man, Jimmy Farrell. He said his father was a farmer a while since, and there's himself now in a poor state. Maybe the land was grabbed from him, and he did what any decent man would do.

MICHAEL [*To Christy, mysteriously*] Was it bailiffs?

CHRISTY The divil a one.

MICHAEL Agents?

CHRISTY The divil a one.

MICHAEL Landlords?

CHRISTY [*Peevishly*] Ah, not at all, I'm saying. You'd

see the like of them stories on any little paper of a
Munster town. But I'm not calling to mind any person,
gentle, simple, judge or jury, did the like of me.

[*They all draw nearer with delighted curiosity*]

PHILLY Well, that lad's a puzzle-the-world.

JIMMY He'd beat Dan Davies's circus, or the holy
missioners making sermons on the villainy of man.
Try him again, Philly.

PHILLY Did you strike golden guineas out of solder,
young fellow, or shilling coins itself?

CHRISTY I did not, mister, not sixpence nor a farthing coin.

JIMMY Did you marry three wives maybe? I'm told
there's a sprinkling have done that among the holy
Luthers of the preaching north.

CHRISTY [*Shyly*] I never married with one, let alone with
a couple or three.   *like Shawn*

PHILLY Maybe he went fighting for the Boers, the like
of the man beyond, was judged to be hanged,
quartered, and drawn. Were you off east, young
fellow, fighting bloody wars for Kruger and the
freedom of the Boers?

CHRISTY I never left my own parish till Tuesday was a
week.

PEGEEN [*Coming from counter*] He's done nothing, so.
[*To Christy*] If you didn't commit murder or a bad,
nasty thing; or false coining, or robbery, or butchery,
or the like of them, there isn't anything that would
be worth your troubling for to run from now. You
did nothing at all.

CHRISTY [*His feelings hurt*] That's an unkindly thing to
be saying to a poor orphaned traveller, has a prison
behind him, and hanging before, and hell's gap gaping
below.

PEGEEN [*With a sign to the men to be quiet*] You're only saying it. You did nothing at all. A soft lad the like of you wouldn't slit the wind pipe of a screeching sow.

CHRISTY [*Offended*] You're not speaking the truth.

PEGEEN [*In mock rage*] Not speaking the truth, is it? Would you have me knock the head of you with the butt of the broom? *reminent of crime*

CHRISTY [*Twisting round on her with a sharp cry of horror*] Don't strike me. I killed my poor father, Tuesday was a week, for doing the like of that.

PEGEEN [*With blank amazement*] Is it killed your father?

CHRISTY [*Subsiding*] With the help of God I did, surely, and that the Holy Immaculate Mother may intercede for his soul. *Ironic — god helps to murder*

PHILLY [*Retreating with Jimmy*] There's a daring fellow.

JIMMY Oh, glory be to God!

MICHAEL [*With great respect*] That was a hanging crime, mister honey. You should have had good reason for doing the like of that.

CHRISTY [*In a very reasonable tone*] He was a dirty man, God forgive him, and he getting old and crusty, the way I couldn't put up with him at all.

PEGEEN And you shot him dead?

CHRISTY [*Shaking his head*] I never used weapons. I've no licence, and I'm a law-fearing man.

MICHAEL It was with a hilted knife maybe? I'm told, in the big world, it's bloody knives they use.

CHRISTY [*Loudly, scandalized*] Do you take me for a slaughter-boy? *murder has to be done in accepted way.*

PEGEEN You never hanged him, the way Jimmy Farrell hanged his dog from the licence, and had it screeching and wriggling three hours at the butt of a string, and

51

himself swearing it was a dead dog, and the peelers
swearing it had life?

CHRISTY I did not, then. I just riz the loy and let fall the
edge of it on the ridge of his skull, and he went down
at my feet like an empty sack, and never let a grunt
or groan from him at all.

MICHAEL [*Making a sign to Pegeen to fill Christy's glass*]
And what way weren't you hanged, mister? Did you
bury him then?

CHRISTY [*Considering*] Aye. I buried him then. Wasn't
I digging spuds in the field?

MICHAEL And the peelers never followed after you the
eleven days that you're out?

CHRISTY [*Shaking his head*] Never a one of them, and I
walking forward facing hog, dog, or divil on the highway of the road.

PHILLY [*Nodding wisely*] It's only with a common week-
day kind of murderer them lads would be trusting their
carcass, and that man should be a great terror when
his temper's roused.

MICHAEL He should then. [*To Christy*] And where was
it, mister honey, that you did the deed?

CHRISTY [*Looking at him with suspicion*] Oh, a distant
place, master of the house, a windy corner of high,
distant hills. *beautifully romantic*

PHILLY [*Nodding with approval*] He's a close man, and
he's right, surely.

PEGEEN That'd be a lad with the sense of Solomon to have
for a pot-boy, Michael James, if it's the truth you're
seeking one at all. *her ideal*

PHILLY The peelers is fearing him, and if you'd that lad
in the house there isn't one of them would come
smelling around if the dogs itself were lapping poteen

from the dung-pit of the yard.

JIMMY Bravery's a treasure in a lonesome place, and a lad would kill his father, I'm thinking, would face a foxy divil with a pitchpike on the flags of hell.

PEGEEN It's the truth they're saying, and if I'd that lad in the house, I wouldn't be fearing the loosèd khaki cut-throats, or the walking dead.

CHRISTY [*Swelling with surprise and triumph*] Well, glory be to God!

MICHAEL [*With deference*] Would you think well to stop here and be pot-boy, mister honey, if we gave you good wages, and didn't destroy you with the weight of work.

SHAWN [*Coming forward uneasily*] That'd be a queer kind to bring into a decent, quiet household with the like of Pegeen Mike.

PEGEEN [*Very sharply*] Will you whisht? Who's speaking to you?

SHAWN [*Retreating*] A bloody-handed murderer the like of . . .   realist motivation is jealousy

PEGEEN [*Snapping at him*] Whisht, I am saying; we'll take no fooling from your like at all. [*To Christy, with a honeyed voice*] And you, young fellow, you'd have a right to stop, I'm thinking, for we'd do our all and utmost to content your needs.

CHRISTY [*Overcome with wonder*] And I'd be safe this place from the searching law?

MICHAEL You would, surely. If they're not fearing you, itself, the peelers in this place is decent, drouthy poor fellows, wouldn't touch a cur dog and not give warning in the dead of night.

PEGEEN [*Very kindly and persuasively*] Let you stop a short while anyhow. Aren't you destroyed by walking with your feet in bleeding blisters, and your whole skin needing washing like a Wicklow sheep.

CHRISTY [*Looking round with satisfaction*] It's a nice room, and if it's not humbugging me you are, I'm thinking that I'll surely stay.

JIMMY [*Jumps up*] Now, by the grace of God, herself will be safe this night, with a man killed his father holding danger from the door, and let you come on, Michael James, or they'll have the best stuff drunk at the wake.

MICHAEL [*Going to the door with men*] And begging your pardon, mister, what name will we call you, for we'd like to know?

CHRISTY Christopher Mahon

MICHAEL Well, God bless you, Christy, and a good rest till we meet again when the sun'll be rising to the noon of the day.

CHRISTY God bless you all.

MEN God bless you.

[*They go out, except Shawn, who lingers at the door*]

SHAWN [*To Pegeen*] Are you wanting me to stop along with you and keep you from harm?

PEGEEN [*Gruffly*] Didn't you say you were fearing Father Reilly? *doesn't need Shawn now*

SHAWN There'd be no harm staying now, I'm thinking, and himself in it too.

PEGEEN You wouldn't stay when there was need for you, and let you step off nimble this time when there's none.

SHAWN Didn't I say it was Father Reilly. . . .

PEGEEN Go on, then, to Father Reilly [*in a jeering tone*], and let him put you in the holy brotherhoods, and leave that lad to me.

SHAWN If I meet the Widow Quin . . .

PEGEEN Go on, I'm saying, and don't be waking this place with your noise. [*She hustles him out and bolts door*] That lad would wear the spirits from the saints of peace. [*Bustles about, then takes off her apron and pins it up in the window as a blind, Christy watching her timidly. Then she comes to him and speaks with bland good humour*] Let you stretch out now by the fire, young fellow. You should be destroyed travelling.

CHRISTY [*Shyly again, drawing off his boots*] I'm tired surely, walking wild eleven days, and waking fearful in the night.

[*He holds up one of his feet, feeling his blisters, and looking at them with compassion*]

PEGEEN [*Standing beside him, watching him with delight*] You should have had great people in your family, I'm thinking, with the little, small feet you have, and you with a kind of a quality name, the like of what you'd find on the great powers and potentates of France and Spain. Totally Irish name   romantic idea

CHRISTY [*With pride*] We were great, surely, with wide and windy acres of rich Munster land.

PEGEEN Wasn't I telling you, and you a fine, handsome young fellow with a noble brow?

CHRISTY [*With a flush of delighted surprise*] Is it me?

PEGEEN Aye. Did you never hear that from the young girls where you come from in the west or south?

CHRISTY [*With venom*] I did not, then. Oh, they're bloody liars in the naked parish where I grew a man.

PEGEEN If they are itself, you've heard it these days, I'm thinking, and you walking the world telling out your story to young girls or old.   wants to find out about Christy jealousy

CHRISTY I've told my story no place till this night, Pegeen Mike, and it's foolish I was here, maybe, to be talking

55

free; but you're decent people, I'm thinking, and
yourself a kindly woman, the way I wasn't fearing
you at all.

PEGEEN [*Filling a sack with straw*] You've said the like
of that, maybe, in every cot and cabin where you've
met a young girl on your way.

CHRISTY [*Going over to her, gradually raising his voice*]
I've said it nowhere till this night, I'm telling you; for
I've seen none the like of you the eleven long days I
am walking the world, looking over a low ditch or a
high ditch on my north or south, into stony, scattered
fields, or scribes of bog, where you'd see young, limber
girls, and fine, prancing women making laughter with
the men.

PEGEEN If you weren't destroyed travelling, you'd have
as much talk and streeleen, I'm thinking, as Owen
Roe O'Sullivan or the poets of the Dingle Bay; and
I've heard all times it's the poets are your like—fine,
fiery fellows with great rages when their temper's
roused.

CHRISTY [*Drawing a little nearer to her*] You've a power
of rings, God bless you, and would there be any
offence if I was asking are you single now?

PEGEEN What would I want wedding so young?

CHRISTY [*With relief*] We're alike so.

PEGEEN [*She puts sack on settle and beats it up*] I never
killed my father. I'd be afeared to do that, except I
was the like of yourself with blind rages tearing me
within, for I'm thinking you should have had great
tussling when the end was come.

CHRISTY [*Expanding with delight at the first confidential
talk he has ever had with a woman*] We had not then.
It was a hard woman was come over the hill; and if he

was always a crusty kind, when he'd a hard woman setting him on, not the divil himself or his four fathers could put up with him at all.

PEGEEN [*With curiosity*] And isn't it a great wonder that one wasn't fearing you?

CHRISTY [*Very confidentially*] Up to the day I killed my father, there wasn't a person in Ireland knew the kind I was, and I there drinking, waking, eating, sleeping, a quiet, simple poor fellow with no man giving me heed.

PEGEEN [*Getting a quilt out of cupboard and putting it on the sack*] It was the girls were giving you heed, maybe, and I'm thinking it's most conceit you'd have to be gaming with their like.

CHRISTY [*Shaking his head with simplicity*] Not the girls itself, and I won't tell you a lie. There wasn't any one heeding me in that place saving only the dumb beasts of the field.

[*He sits down at fire*]

PEGEEN [*With disappointment*] And I thinking you should have been living the like of a king of Norway or the eastern world.

[*She comes and sits beside him after placing bread and mug of milk on the table*]

CHRISTY [*Laughing piteously*] The like of a king, is it? And I after toiling, moiling, digging, dodging from the dawn till dusk; with never a sight of joy or sport saving only when I'd be abroad in the dark night poaching rabbits on hills, for I was a divil to poach, God forgive me [*very naïvely*], and I near got six months for going with a dung fork and stabbing a fish.

PEGEEN And it's that you'd call sport, is it, to be abroad in the darkness with yourself alone?

57

CHRISTY I did, God help me, and there I'd be as happy
as the sunshine of St. Martin's Day, watching the light
passing the north or the patches of fog, till I'd hear
a rabbit starting to screech and I'd go running in the
furze. Then, when I'd my full share, I'd come walking
down where you'd see the ducks and geese stretched
sleeping on the highway of the road, and before I'd
pass the dunghill, I'd hear himself snoring out—a loud,
lonesome snore he'd be making all times, the while
he was sleeping; and he a man'd be raging all times,
the while he was waking, like a gaudy officer you'd
hear cursing and damning and swearing oaths.

PEGEEN Providence and Mercy, spare us all!

CHRISTY It's that you'd say surely if you seen him and he
after drinking for weeks, rising up in the red dawn,
or before it maybe, and going out into the yard as
naked as an ash-tree in the moon of May, and shying
clods against the visage of the stars till he'd put the
fear of death into the banbhs and the screeching sows.

PEGEEN I'd be well-nigh afeard of that lad myself, I'm
thinking. And there was no one in it but the two of
you alone?

CHRISTY The divil a one, though he'd sons and daughters
walking all great states and territories of the world,
and not a one of them, to this day, but would say their
seven curses on him, and they rousing up to let a cough
or sneeze, maybe, in the deadness of the night.

PEGEEN [Nodding her head] Well, you should have been
a queer lot. I never cursed my father the like of that,
though I'm twenty and more years of age.

CHRISTY Then you'd have cursed mine, I'm telling you,
and he a man never gave peace to any, saving when
he'd get two months or three, or be locked in the

58

asylums for battering peelers or assaulting men [*with depression*], the way it was a bitter life he led me till I did up a Tuesday and halve his skull.

PEGEEN [*Putting her hand on his shoulder*] Well, you'll have peace in this place, Christy Mahon, and none to trouble you, and it's near time a fine lad like you should have your good share of the earth.

CHRISTY It's time surely, and I a seemly fellow with great strength in me and bravery of . . .

[*Someone knocks*]

CHRISTY [*Clinging to Pegeen*] Oh, glory! it's late for knocking, and this last while I'm in terror of the peelers, and the walking dead.

[*Knocking again*]

PEGEEN Who's there?

VOICE [*Outside*] Me.

PEGEEN Who's me?

VOICE The Widow Quin.

PEGEEN [*Jumping up and giving him the bread and milk*] Go on now with your supper, and let on to be sleepy, for if she found you were such a warrant to talk, she'd be stringing gabble till the dawn of day.

[*He takes bread and sits shyly with his back to the door*]

PEGEEN [*Opening door, with temper*] What ails you, or what is it you're wanting at this hour of the night?

WIDOW QUIN [*Coming in a step and peering at Christy*] I'm after meeting Shawn Keogh and Father Reilly below, who told me of your curiosity man, and they fearing by this time he was roaring, romping on your hands with drink.

PEGEEN [*Pointing to Christy*] Look now is he roaring, and he stretched out drowsy with his supper and his

59

mug of milk. Walk down and tell that to Father Reilly and to Shaneen Keogh.

WIDOW QUIN [*Coming forward*] I'll not see them again, for I've their word to lead that lad forward to lodge with me.

PEGEEN [*In blank amazement*] This night is it?

WIDOW QUIN [*Going over*] This night. 'It isn't fitting,' says the priesteen, 'to have his likeness lodging with an orphaned girl.' [*To Christy*] God save you mister!

CHRISTY [*Shyly*] God save you kindly!

WIDOW QUIN [*Looking at him with half amused curiosity*] Well, aren't you a little smiling fellow? It should have been great and bitter torments did rouse your spirits to a deed of blood.

CHRISTY [*Doubtfully*] It should, maybe.

WIDOW QUIN It's more than 'maybe' I'm saying, and it'd soften my heart to see you sitting so simple with your cup and cake, and you fitter to be saying your catechism than slaying your da.

PEGEEN [*At counter, washing glasses*] There's talking when any'd see he's fit to be holding his head high with the wonders of the world. Walk on from this, for I'll not have him tormented, and he destroyed travelling since Tuesday was a week.

WIDOW QUIN [*Peaceably*] We'll be walking surely when his supper's done, and you'll find we're great company, young fellow, when it's of the like of you and me you'd hear the penny poets singing in an August Fair.

CHRISTY [*Innocently*] Did you kill your father?

PEGEEN [*Contemptuously*] She did not. She hit himself with a worn pick, and the rusted poison did corrode his blood the way he never overed it, and died after. That was a sneaky kind of murder did win small glory with the boys itself.

[*She crosses to Christy's left*]

WIDOW QUIN [*With good humour*] If it didn't, maybe all knows a widow woman has buried her children and destroyed her man is a wiser comrade for a young lad than a girl, the like of you, who'd go helter-skeltering after any man would let you a wink upon the road.

PEGEEN [*Breaking out into wild rage*] And you'll say that, Widow Quin, and you gasping with the rage you had *man hungry* racing the hill beyond to look on his face.

WIDOW QUIN [*Laughing derisively*] Me, is it? Well, Father Reilly has cuteness to divide you now. [*She pulls Christy up*] There's great temptation in a man did slay his da, and we'd best be going, young fellow; so rise up and come with me.

PEGEEN [*Seizing his arm*] He'll not stir. He's pot-boy in this place, and I'll not have him stolen off and kidnapped while himself's abroad.

WIDOW QUIN It'd be a crazy pot-boy'd lodge him in the shebeen where he works by day, so you'd have a right to come on, young fellow, till you see my little houseen, a perch off on the rising hill.

PEGEEN Wait till morning, Christy Mahon. Wait till you lay eyes on her leaky thatch is growing more pasture for her buck goat than her square of fields, and she without a tramp itself to keep in order her place at all.

WIDOW QUIN When you see me contriving in my little gardens, Christy Mahon, you'll swear the Lord God formed me to be living lone, and that there isn't my match in Mayo for thatching, or mowing, or shearing a sheep.

PEGEEN [*With noisy scorn*] It's true the Lord God formed you to contrive indeed. Doesn't the world know you

[handwritten margin note: exaggerated folk tale]

reared a black ram at your own breast, so that the Lord Bishop of Connaught felt the elements of a Christian, and he eating it after in a kidney stew? Doesn't the world know you've been seen shaving the foxy skipper from France for a threepenny-bit and a sop of grass tobacco would wring the liver from a mountain goat you'd meet leaping the hills? *[handwritten: Kind of witch]*

WIDOW QUIN [*With amusement*] Do you hear her now, young fellow? Do you hear the way she'll be rating at your own self when a week is by?

PEGEEN [*To Christy*] Don't heed her. Tell her to go on into her pigsty and not plague us here.

WIDOW QUIN I'm going; but he'll come with me.

PEGEEN [*Shaking him*] Are you dumb, young fellow?

CHRISTY [*Timidly to Widow Quin*] God increase you; but I'm pot-boy in this place, and it's here I liefer stay.

PEGEEN [*Triumphantly*] Now you have heard him, and go on from this.

WIDOW QUIN [*Looking round the room*] It's lonesome this hour crossing the hill, and if he won't come along with me, I'd have a right maybe to stop this night with yourselves. Let me stretch out on the settle, Pegeen Mike; and himself can lie by the hearth.

PEGEEN [*Short and fiercely*] Faith, I won't. Quit off or I will send you now.

WIDOW QUIN [*Gathering her shawl up*] Well, it's a terror to be aged a score. *[handwritten: 20 yrs.]* [*To Christy*] God bless you now, young fellow, and let you be wary, or there's right torment will await you here if you go romancing with her like, and she waiting only, as they bade me say, on a sheepskin parchment to be wed with Shawn Keogh of Killakeen. *[handwritten: right warning]*

CHRISTY [*Going to Pegeen as she bolts door*] What's that

62

she's after saying?

PEGEEN Lies and blather, you've no call to mind. Well, isn't Shawn Keogh an impudent fellow to send up spying on me? Wait till I lay hands on him. Let him wait, I'm saying.

CHRISTY And you're not wedding him at all?

PEGEEN I wouldn't wed him if a bishop came walking for to join us here.

CHRISTY That God in glory may be thanked for that.

PEGEEN There's your bed now. I've put a quilt upon you I'm after quilting a while since with my own two hands, and you'd best stretch out now for your sleep, and may God give you a good rest till I call you in the morning when the cocks will crow.

CHRISTY [*As she goes to inner room*] May God and Mary and St. Patrick bless you and reward you for your kindly talk. [*She shuts the door behind her. He settles his bed slowly, feeling the quilt with immense satisfaction*] Well, it's a clean bed and soft with it, and it's great luck and company I've won me in the end of time—two fine women fighting for the likes of me— till I'm thinking this night wasn't I a foolish fellow not to kill my father in the years gone by.

CURTAIN

ACT II

Scene as before. Brilliant morning light. Christy, looking bright and cheerful, is cleaning a girl's boots.

CHRISTY [*To himself, counting jugs on dresser*] Half a hundred beyond. Ten there. A score that's above. Eighty jugs. Six cups and a broken one. Two plates. A power of glasses. Bottles, a schoolmaster'd be hard set to count, and enough in them, I'm thinking, to drunken all the wealth and wisdom of the county Clare. [*He puts down the boot carefully*] There's her boots now, nice and decent for her evening use, and isn't it grand brushes she has? [*He puts them down and goes by degrees to the looking-glass*] Well, this'd be a fine place to be my whole life talking out with swearing Christians, in place of my old dogs and cat; and I stalking around, smoking my pipe and drinking my fill, and never a day's work but drawing a cork an odd time, or wiping a glass, or rinsing out a shiny tumbler for a decent man. [*He takes the looking-glass from the wall and puts it on the back of a chair; then sits down in front of it and begins washing his face*] Didn't I know rightly, I was handsome, though it was the divil's own mirror we had beyond, would twist a squint across an angel's brow; and I'll be growing fine from this day, the way I'll have a soft lovely skin on me and won't be the like of the clumsy young fellows do be ploughing all times in the earth and dung. [*He starts*] Is she coming again? [*He looks out*] Stranger

64

girls. God help me, where'll I hide myself away and my long neck naked to the world? [*He looks out*] I'd best go to the room maybe till I'm dressed again.

[*He gathers up his coat and the looking-glass, and runs into the inner room. The door is pushed open, and Susan Brady looks in, and knocks on door*]

SUSAN There's nobody in it. [*Knocks again*]

NELLY [*Pushing her in and following her, with Honor Blake and Sara Tansey*] It'd be early for them both to be out walking the hill.

SUSAN I'm thinking Shawn Keogh was making game of us, and there's no such man in it at all.

HONOR [*Pointing to straw and quilt*] Look at that. He's been sleeping there in the night. Well, it'll be a hard case if he's gone off now, the way we'll never set our eyes on a man killed his father, and we after rising early and destroying ourselves running fast on the hill.

NELLY Are you thinking them's his boots?

SARAH [*Taking them up*] If they are, there should be his father's track on them. Did you never read in the papers the way murdered men do bleed and drip?

SUSAN Is that blood there, Sara Tansey?

SARA [*Smelling it*] That's bog water, I'm thinking; but it's his own they are, surely, for I never seen the like of them for whitey mud, and red mud, and turf on them, and the fine sands of the sea. That man's been walking, I'm telling you.

[*She goes down right, putting on one of his boots*]

SUSAN [*Going to window*] Maybe he's stolen off to Belmullet with the boots of Michael James, and you'd have a right so to follow after him, Sara Tansey, and you the one yoked the ass-cart and drove ten miles to set your eyes on the man bit the yellow lady's nostril on the northern shore. [*She looks out*]

SARA [*Running to window, with one boot on*] Don't be talking, and we fooled today. [*Putting on the other boot*] There's a pair do fit me well and I'll be keeping them for walking to the priest, when you'd be ashamed this place, going up winter and summer with nothing worth while to confess at all.

HONOR [*Who has been listening at door*] Whisht! there's someone inside the room. [*She pushes door a chink open*] It's a man.

[*Sara kicks off boots and puts them where they were. They all stand in a line looking through chink*]

SARA I'll call him. Mister! Mister! [*He puts in his head*] Is Pegeen within?

CHRISTY [*Coming in as meek as a mouse, with the looking-glass held behind his back*] She's above on the cnuceen, seeking the nanny goats, the way she'd have a sup of goats' milk for to colour my tea.

SARA And asking your pardon, is it you's the man killed his father?

CHRISTY [*Sidling toward the nail where the glass was hanging*] I am, God help me!

SARA [*Taking eggs she has brought*] Then my thousand welcomes to you, and I've run up with a brace of duck's eggs for your food today. Pegeen's ducks is no use, but these are the real rich sort. Hold out your hand and you'll see it's no lie I'm telling you.

CHRISTY [*Coming foward shyly, and holding out his left hand*] They're a great and weighty size.

SUSAN And I run up with a pat of butter, for it'd be a poor thing to have you eating your spuds dry, and you after running a great way since you did destroy your da.

CHRISTY Thank you kindly.

HONOR And I brought you a little cut of a cake, for you should have a thin stomach on you, and you that length walking the world.

NELLY And I brought you a little laying pullet—boiled and all she is—was crushed at the fall of night by the curate's car. Feel the fat of the breast, mister.

CHRISTY It's bursting, surely.

[*He feels it with the back of his hand, in which he holds the presents*]

SARA Will you pinch it? Is your right hand too sacred for to use at all? [*She slips round behind him*] It's a glass he has. Well, I never seen to this day a man with a looking-glass held to his back. Them that kills their fathers is a vain lot surely. [*Girls giggle*]

CHRISTY [*Smiling innocently and piling presents on glass*] I'm very thankful to you all today. . . .

WIDOW QUIN [*Coming in quietly, at door*] Sara Tansey, Susan Brady, Honor Blake! What in glory has you here at this hour of day!

GIRLS [*Giggling*] That's the man killed his father.

WIDOW QUIN [*Coming to them*] I know well it's the man; and I'm after putting him down in the sports below for racing, leaping, pitching, and the Lord knows what.

SARA [*Exuberantly*] That's right, Widow Quin. I'll bet my dowry that he'll lick the world.

WIDOW QUIN If you will, you'd have a right to have him fresh and nourished in place of nursing a feast. [*Taking presents*] Are you fasting or fed, young fellow?

CHRISTY Fasting, if you please.

WIDOW QUIN [*Loudly*] Well, you're the lot. Stir up now and give him his breakfast. [*To Christy*] Come here to me [*she puts him on bench beside her while the girls make tea and get his breakfast*], and let you tell us your story before Pegeen will come, in place of grinning your ears off like the moon of May.

CHRISTY [*Beginning to be pleased*] It's a long story; you'd be destroyed listening.

WIDOW QUIN Don't be letting on to be shy, a fine, gamy, treacherous lad the like of you. Was it in your house beyond you cracked his skull?

CHRISTY [*Shy but flattered*] It was not. We were digging spuds in his cold, sloping, stony, divil's patch of a field.

WIDOW QUIN And you went asking money of him, or making talk of getting a wife would drive him from his farm?

CHRISTY I did not, then; but there I was, digging and digging, and 'You squinting idot,' says he, 'let you walk down now and tell the priest you'll wed the Widow Casey in a score of days.'

WIDOW QUIN And what kind was she?

CHRISTY [*With horror*] A walking terror from beyond the hills, and she two score and five years, and two hundred weights and five pounds in the weighing scales, with a limping leg on her, and a blinded eye, and she a woman of noted misbehaviour with the old and young.

GIRLS [*Clustering round him, serving him*] Glory be.

WIDOW QUIN And what did he want driving you to wed with her? [*She takes a bit of the chicken*]

CHRISTY [*Eating with growing satisfaction*] He was letting on I was wanting a protector from the harshness of the world, and he without a thought the whole while but how he'd have her hut to live in and her gold to drink.

68

WIDOW QUIN There's maybe worse than a dry hearth and a widow woman and your glass at night. So you hit him then?

CHRISTY [*Getting almost excited*] I did not. 'I won't wed her,' says I, 'when all know she did suckle me for six weeks when I came into the world, and she a hag this day with a tongue on her has the crows and seabirds scattered, the way they wouldn't cast a shadow on her garden with the dread of her curse.'

WIDOW QUIN [*Teasingly*] That one should be right company.

SARA [*Eagerly*] Don't mind her. Did you kill him then?

CHRISTY 'She's too good for the like of you,' says he, 'and go on now or I'll flatten you out like a crawling beast has passed under a dray.' 'You will not if I can help it,' says I. 'Go on,' says he, 'or I'll have the divil making garters of your limbs tonight.' 'You will not if I can help it,' says I. [*He sits up brandishing his mug*]

SARA You were right surely.

CHRISTY [*Impressively*] With that the sun came out between the cloud and the hill, and it shining green in my face. 'God have mercy on your soul,' says he, lifting a scythe. 'Or on your own,' says I, raising the loy.

SUSAN That's a grand story.

HONOR He tells it lovely.

CHRISTY [*Flattered and confident, waving bone*] He gave a drive with the scythe, and I gave a lep to the east. Then I turned around with my back to the north, and I hit a blow on the ridge of his skull, laid him stretched out, and he split to the knob of his gullet.

[*He raises the chicken bone to his Adam's apple*]

GIRLS [*Together*] Well, you're a marvel! Oh, God bless you! You're the lad, surely!

69

SUSAN I'm thinking the Lord God sent him this road to make a second husband to the Widow Quin, and she with a great yearning to be wedded, though all dread her here. Lift him on her knee, Sara Tansey.

WIDOW QUIN Don't tease him.

SARA [*Going over to dresser and counter very quickly and getting two glasses and porter*] You're heroes, surely, and let you drink a supeen with your arms linked like the outlandish lovers in the sailor's song. [*She links their arms and gives them the glasses*] There now. Drink a health to the wonders of the western world, the pirates, preachers, poteen-makers, with the jobbing jockies; parching peelers, and the juries fill their stomachs selling judgments of the English law. [*Brandishing the bottle*]

WIDOW QUIN That's a right toast, Sara Tansey. Now, Christy.

[*They drink with their arms linked, he drinking with his left hand, she with her right. As they are drinking, Pegeen Mike comes in with a milk-can and stands aghast. They all spring away from Christy. He goes down left. Widow Quin remains seated*]

PEGEEN [*Angrily to Sara*] What is it you're wanting?

SARA [*Twisting her apron*] An ounce of tobacco.

PEGEEN Have you tuppence?

SARA I've forgotten my purse.

PEGEEN Then you'd best be getting it and not be fooling us here. [*To the Widow Quin, with more elaborate scorn*] And what is it you're wanting, Widow Quin?

WIDOW QUIN [*Insolently*] A penn'orth of starch.

PEGEEN [*Breaking out*] And you without a white shift or a shirt in your whole family since the dying of the flood. I've no starch for the like of you, and let you walk on now to Killamuck.

WIDOW QUIN [*Turning to Christy, as she goes out with the girls*] Well, you're mighty huffy this day, Pegeen Mike, and you, young fellow, let you not forget the sports and racing when the noon is by. [*They go out*]

PEGEEN [*Imperiously*] Fling out that rubbish and put them cups away. [*Christy tidies away in great haste*] Shove in the bench by the wall. [*He does so*] And hang that glass on the nail. What disturbed it at all?

CHRISTY [*Very meekly*] I was making myself decent only, and this a fine country for young lovely girls.

PEGEEN [*Sharply*] Whisht your talking of girls. [*Goes to counter on right*]

CHRISTY Wouldn't any wish to be decent in a place . . .

PEGEEN Whisht, I'm saying.

CHRISTY [*Looks at her face for a moment with great misgivings, then as a last effort takes up a loy, and goes towards her, with feigned assurance*] It was with a loy the like of that I killed my father.

PEGEEN [*Still sharply*] You've told me that story six times since the dawn of day. *no accurate knows what Christy is like*

CHRISTY [*Reproachfully*] It's a queer thing you wouldn't care to be hearing it and them girls after walking four miles to be listening to me now.

PEGEEN [*Turning round astonished*] Four miles?

CHRISTY [*Apologetically*] Didn't himself say there were only bona fides living in the place?

PEGEEN It's bona fides by the road they are, but that lot came over the river lepping the stones. It's not three perches when you go like that, and I was down this morning looking on the papers the post-boy does have in his bag. [*With meaning and emphasis*] For there was great news this day, Christopher Mahon. [*She goes into room on left*]

CHRISTY [*Suspiciously*] Is it news of my murder?

PEGEEN [*Inside*] Murder, indeed.

CHRISTY [*Loudly*] A murdered da?

PEGEEN [*Coming in again and crossing right*] There was not, but a story filled half a page of the hanging of a man. Ah, that should be a fearful end, young fellow, and it worst of all for a man destroyed his da; for the like of him would get small mercies, and when it's dead he is they'd put him in a narrow grave, with cheap sacking wrapping him round, and pour down quick-lime on his head, the way you'd see a woman pouring any frish-frash from a cup.

CHRISTY [*Very miserably*] Oh, God help me. Are you thinking I'm safe? You were saying at the fall of night I was shut of jeopardy and I here with yourselves.

PEGEEN [*Severely*] You'll be shut of jeopardy no place if you go talking with a pack of wild girls the like of them do be walking abroad with the peelers, talking whispers at the fall of night.

CHRISTY [*With terror*] And you're thinking they'd tell?

PEGEEN [*With mock sympathy*] Who knows, God help you?

CHRISTY [*Loudly*] What joy would they have to bring hanging to the likes of me?

PEGEEN It's queer joys they have, and who knows the thing they'd do, if it'd make the green stones cry itself to think of you swaying and swinging at the butt of a rope, and you with a fine, stout neck, God bless you! the way you'd be a half an hour, in great anguish, getting your death.

CHRISTY [*Getting his boots and putting them on*] If there's

72

that terror of them, it'd be best, maybe, I went on
wandering like Esau or Cain and Abel on the sides of
Neifin or the Erris plain.

PEGEEN [*Beginning to play with him*] It would, maybe,
for I've heard the circuit judges this place is a heartless
crew.

CHRISTY [*Bitterly*] It's more than judges this place is a
heartless crew. [*Looking up at her*] And isn't it a poor
thing to be starting again, and I a lonesome fellow will
be looking out on women and girls the way the needy
fallen spirits do be looking on the Lord?

PEGEEN What call have you to be that lonesome when
there's poor girls walking Mayo in their thousands
now?

CHRISTY [*Grimly*] It's well you know what call I have.
It's well you know it's a lonesome thing to be passing
small towns with the lights shining sideways when the
night is down, or going in strange places with a dog
noising before you and a dog noising behind, or drawn
to the cities where you'd hear a voice kissing and talking deep love in every shadow of the ditch, and you
passing on with an empty, hungry stomach failing
from your heart.

*wandering
hero*

PEGEEN I'm thinking you're an odd man, Christy Mahon.
The oddest walking fellow I ever set my eyes on to this
hour today.

CHRISTY What would any be but odd men and they living
lonesome in the world?

PEGEEN I'm not odd, and I'm my whole life with my
father only.

CHRISTY [*With infinite admiration*] How would a lovely,
handsome woman the like of you be lonesome when
all men should be thronging around to hear the sweet-

73

ness of your voice, and the little infant children should
be pestering your steps, I'm thinking, and you walking
the roads.

PEGEEN I'm hard set to know what way a coaxing fellow
the like of yourself should be lonesome either.

CHRISTY Coaxing?

PEGEEN Would you have me think a man never talked
with the girls would have the words you've spoken today? It's only letting on you are to be lonesome, the
way you'd get around me now.

CHRISTY I wish to God I was letting on; but I was lonesome all times, and born lonesome, I'm thinking, as the
moon of dawn. like St. Joan

[*Going to door*]

PEGEEN [*Puzzled by his talk*] Well, it's a story I'm not
understanding at all why you'd be worse than another,
Christy Mahon, and you a fine lad with the great
savagery to destroy your da.

CHRISTY It's little I'm understanding myself, saving only
that my heart's scalded this day, and I going off stretching out the earth between us, the way I'll not be
waking near you another dawn of the year till the two
of us do arise to hope or judgment with the saints of
God, and now I'd best be going with my wattle in my
hand, for hanging is a poor thing [*turning to go*], and
it's little welcome only is left me in this house today.

PEGEEN [*Sharply*] Christy. [*He turns round*] Come here
to me. [*He goes towards her*] Lay down that switch
and throw some sods on the fire. You're pot-boy in
this place, and I'll not have you mitch off from us now.

CHRISTY You were saying I'd be hanged if I stay.

PEGEEN [*Quite kindly at last*] I'm after going down and
reading the fearful crimes of Ireland for two weeks or

three, and there wasn't a word of your murder. [*Getting up and going over to the counter*] They've likely not found the body. You're safe so with ourselves.

CHRISTY [*Astonished, slowly*] It's making game of me you were [*following her with fearful joy*], and I can stay so, working at your side, and I not lonesome from this mortal day.

PEGEEN What's to hinder you staying, except the widow woman or the young girls would inveigle you off?

CHRISTY [*With rapture*] And I'll have your words from this day filling my ears, and that look is come upon you meeting my two eyes, and I watching you loafing around in the warm sun, or rinsing your ankles when the night is come.

PEGEEN [*Kindly, but a little embarrassed*] I'm thinking you'll be a loyal young lad to have working around, and if you vexed me a while since with your leaguing with the girls, I wouldn't give a thraneen for a lad hadn't a mighty spirit in him and a gamy heart.

[*Shawn Keogh runs in carrying a cleeve on his back, followed by the Widow Quin*]

SHAWN [*To Pegeen*] I was passing below, and I seen your mountainy sheep eating cabbages in Jimmy's field. Run up or they'll be bursting surely.

PEGEEN Oh, God mend them!

[*She puts a shawl over her head and runs out*]

CHRISTY [*Looking from one to the other. Still in high spirits*] I'd best go to her aid maybe. I'm handy with ewes. *Afraid of being left*

WIDOW QUIN [*Closing the door*] She can do that much, and there is Shaneen has long speeches for to tell you now. [*She sits down with an amused smile*]

75

SHAWN [*Taking something from his pocket and offering it to Christy*] Do you see that, mister?

CHRISTY [*Looking at it*] The half of a ticket to the Western States!

SHAWN [*Trembling with anxiety*] I'll give it to you and my new hat [*pulling it out of hamper*]; and my breeches with the double seat [*pulling it out*]; and my new coat is woven from the blackest shearings for three miles around [*giving him the coat*]; I'll give you the whole of them, and my blessing, and the blessing of Father Reilly itself, maybe, if you'll quit from this and leave us in the peace we had till last night at the fall of dark.

CHRISTY [*With a new arrogance*] And for what is it you're wanting to get shut of me?

SHAWN [*Looking to the Widow for help*] I'm a poor scholar with middling faculties to coin a lie, so I'll tell you the truth, Christy Mahon. I'm wedding with Pegeen beyond, and I don't think well of having a clever fearless man the like of you dwelling in her house.

CHRISTY [*Almost pugnaciously*] And you'd be using bribery for to banish me?

SHAWN [*In an imploring voice*] Let you not take it badly, mister honey; isn't beyond the best place for you, where you'll have golden chains and shiny coats and you riding upon hunters with the ladies of the land.

[*He makes an eager sign to the Widow Quin to come to help him*]

WIDOW QUIN [*Coming over*] It's true for him, and you'd best quit off and not have that poor girl setting her mind on you, for there's Shaneen thinks she wouldn't suit you, though all is saying that she'll wed you now.

[*Christy beams with delight*]

SHAWN [*In terrified earnest*] She wouldn't suit you, and she with the divil's own temper the way you'd be strangling one another in a score of days. [*He makes the movement of strangling with his hands*] It's the like of me only that she's fit for; a quiet simple fellow wouldn't raise a hand upon her if she scratched itself.

WIDOW QUIN [*Putting Shawn's hat on Christy*] Fit them clothes on you anyhow, young fellow, and he'd maybe loan them to you for the sports. [*Pushing him towards inner door*] Fit them on and you can give your answer when you have them tried.

CHRISTY [*Beaming, delighted with the clothes*] I will then. I'd like herself to see me in them tweeds and hat.

[*He goes into room and shuts the door*]

SHAWN [*In great anxiety*] He'd like herself to see them. He'll not leave us, Widow Quin. He's a score of divils in him the way it's well-nigh certain he will wed Pegeen.

WIDOW QUIN [*Jeeringly*] It's true all girls are fond of courage and do hate the like of you.

SHAWN [*Walking about in desperation*] Oh, Widow Quin, what'll I be doing now? I'd inform again him, but he'd burst from Kilmainham and he'd be sure and certain to destroy me. If I wasn't so God-fearing, I'd near have courage to come behind him and run a pike into his side. Oh, it's a hard case to be an orphan and not to have your father that you're used to, and you'd easy kill and make yourself a hero in the sight of all. [*Coming up to her*] Oh, Widow Quin, will you find me some contrivance when I've promised you a ewe?

WIDOW QUIN A ewe's a small thing, but what would you give me if I did wed him and did save you so?

SHAWN [*With astonishment*] You?

WIDOW QUIN Aye. Would you give me the red cow you have and the mountainy ram, and the right of way across your rye path, and a load of dung at Michaelmas, and turbary upon the western hill?

SHAWN [*Radiant with hope*] I would, surely, and I'd give you the wedding-ring I have, and the loan of a new suit, the way you'd have him decent on the wedding-day. I'd give you two kids for your dinner, and a gallon of poteen, and I'd call the piper on the long car to your wedding from Crossmolina or from Ballina. I'd give you . . .

WIDOW QUIN That'll do, so, and let you whisht, for he's coming now again.

[*Christy comes in, very natty in the new clothes. Widow Quin goes to him admiringly*]

WIDOW QUIN If you seen yourself now, I'm thinking you'd be too proud to speak to at all, and it'd be a pity surely to have your like sailing from Mayo to the western world.

CHRISTY [*As proud as a peacock*] I'm not going. If this is a poor place itself, I'll make myself contented to be lodging here.

[*Widow Quin makes a sign to Shawn to leave them*]

SHAWN Well, I'm going measuring the racecourse while the tide is low, so I'll leave you the garments and my blessing for the sports today. God bless you!

[*He wriggles out*]

WIDOW QUIN [*Admiring Christy*] Well, you're mighty spruce, young fellow. Sit down now while you're quiet till you talk with me.

CHRISTY [*Swaggering*] I'm going abroad on the hillside for to seek Pegeen.

WIDOW QUIN You'll have time and plenty for to seek

Pegeen, and you heard me saying at the fall of night the two of us should be great company.

CHRISTY From this out I'll have no want of company when all sorts is bringing me their food and clothing [*he swaggers to the door, tightening his belt*], the way they'd set their eyes upon a gallant orphan cleft his father with one blow to the breeches belt. [*He opens door, then staggers back*] Saints of Glory! Holy angels from the throne of light!

WIDOW QUIN [*Going over*] What ails you?

CHRISTY It's the walking spirit of my murdered da!

WIDOW QUIN [*Looking out*] Is it that tramper?

CHRISTY [*Wildly*] Where'll I hide my poor body from that ghost of hell?

[*The door is pushed open, and old Mahon appears on threshold. Christy darts in behind door*] Shawn action

WIDOW QUIN [*In great amazement*] God save you, my poor man.

MAHON [*Gruffly*] Did you see a young lad passing this way in the early morning or the fall of night?

WIDOW QUIN You're a queer kind to walk in not saluting at all.

MAHON Did you see the young lad?

WIDOW QUIN [*Stiffly*] What kind was he?

MAHON An ugly young streeler with a murderous gob on him, and a little switch in his hand. I met a tramper seen him coming this way at the fall of night.

WIDOW QUIN There's harvest hundreds do be passing these days for the Sligo boat. For what is it you're wanting him, my poor man?

MAHON I want to destroy him for breaking the head on me with the clout of a loy. [*He takes off a big hat, and shows his head in a mass of bandages and plaster, with*

79   proud of being hurt

some pride] It was he did that, and amn't I a great
wonder to think I've traced him ten days with that
rent in my crown?

WIDOW QUIN [*Taking his head in both hands and examin-
ing it with extreme delight*] That was a great blow.
And who hit you? A robber maybe?

MAHON It was my own son hit me, and he the divil a
robber, or anything else, but a dirty, stuttering lout.

WIDOW QUIN [*Letting go his skull and wiping her hands in
her apron*] You'd best be wary of a mortified scalp, I
think they call it, lepping around with that wound in
the splendour of the sun. It was a bad blow, surely, and
you should have vexed him fearful to make him strike
that gash in his da.

MAHON Is it me?

WIDOW QUIN [*Amusing herself*] Aye. And isn't it a great
shame when the old and hardened do torment the
young?

MAHON [*Raging*] Torment him, is it? And I after holding
out with the patience of a martyred saint till there's
nothing but destruction on, and I'm driven out in my
old age with none to aid me.

WIDOW QUIN [*Greatly amused*] It's a sacred wonder the
way that wickedness will spoil a man.

MAHON My wickedness, is it? Amn't I after saying it is
himself has me destroyed, and he a liar on walls, a
talker of folly, a man you'd see stretched the half of the
day in the brown ferns with his belly to the sun.

WIDOW QUIN Not working at all?

MAHON The divil a work, or if he did itself, you'd see him
raising up a haystack like the stalk of a rush, or driving
our last cow till he broke her leg at the hip, and when
he wasn't at that he'd be fooling over little birds he had

80

—finches and felts—or making mugs at his own self in the bit of glass we had hung on the wall.

WIDOW QUIN [*Looking at Christy*] What way was he so foolish? It was running wild after the girls maybe?

MAHON [*With a shout of derision*] Running wild, is it? If he seen a red petticoat coming swinging over the hill, he'd be off to hide in the sticks, and you'd see him shooting out his sheep's eyes between the little twigs and the leaves, and his two ears rising like a hare looking out through a gap. Girls, indeed!

WIDOW QUIN It was drink maybe?

MAHON And he a poor fellow would get drunk on the smell of a pint. He'd a queer rotten stomach, I'm telling you, and when I gave him three pulls from my pipe a while since, he was taken with contortions till I had to send him in the ass-cart to the females' nurse.

WIDOW QUIN [*Clasping her hands*] Well, I never, till this day, heard tell of a man the like of that!

MAHON I'd take a mighty oath you didn't, surely, and wasn't he the laughing joke of every female woman where four baronies meet, the way the girls would stop their weeding if they seen him coming the road to let a roar at him, and call him the loony of Mahon's?

WIDOW QUIN I'd give the world and all to see the like of him. What kind was he?

MAHON A small, low fellow.

WIDOW QUIN And dark?

MAHON Dark and dirty.

WIDOW QUIN [*Considering*] I'm thinking I seen him.

MAHON [*Eagerly*] An ugly young blackguard.

WIDOW QUIN A hideous, fearful villain, and the spit of you.

MAHON Which way is he fled?

WIDOW QUIN Gone over the hills to catch a coasting steamer to the north or south.

MAHON Could I pull up on him now?

WIDOW QUIN If you'll cross the sands below where the tide is out, you'll be in it as soon as himself, for he had to go round ten miles by the top of the bay. [*She points to the door*] Strike down by the head beyond and then follow on the roadway to the north and east. [*Mahon goes abruptly*]

WIDOW QUIN [*Shouting after him*] Let you give him a good vengeance when you come up with him, but don't put yourself in the power of the law, for it'd be a poor thing to see a judge in his black cap reading out his sentence on a civil warrior the like of you. [*She swings the door to and looks at Christy, who is cowering in terror, for a moment, then she bursts into a laugh*] Well, you're the walking Playboy of the Western World, and that's the poor man you had divided to his breeches belt.

CHRISTY [*Looking out; then, to her*] What'll Pegeen say when she hears that story? What'll she be saying to me now?

WIDOW QUIN She'll knock the head of you, I'm thinking, and drive you from the door. God help her to be taking you for a wonder, and you a little schemer making up a story you destroyed your da.

CHRISTY [*Turning to the door, nearly speechless with rage, half to himself*] To be letting on he was dead, and coming back to his life, and following after me like an old weasel tracing a rat, and coming in here laying desolation between my own self and the fine women of Ireland, and he a kind of carcass that you'd fling upon the sea . . .

WIDOW QUIN [*More soberly*] There's talking for a man's one only son.

CHRISTY [*Breaking out*] His one son, is it? May I meet him with one tooth and it aching, and one eye to be seeing seven and seventy divils in the twists of the road, and one old timber leg on him to limp into the scalding grave. [*Looking out*] There he is now crossing the strands, and that the Lord God would send a high wave to wash him from the world.

WIDOW QUIN [*Scandalized*] Have you no shame? [*Putting her hand on his shoulder and turning him round*] What ails you? Near crying, is it?

CHRISTY [*In despair and grief*] Amn't I after seeing the love-light of the star of knowledge shining from her brow, and hearing words would put you thinking of the holy Brigid speaking to the infant saints, and now she'll be turning again, and speaking hard words to me, like an old woman with a spavindy ass she'd have, urging on a hill.

WIDOW QUIN There's poetry talk for a girl you'd see itching and scratching, and she with a stale stink of poteen on her from selling in the shop.

CHRISTY [*Impatiently*] It's her like is fitted to be handling merchandise in the heavens above, and what'll I be doing now, I ask you, and I a kind of wonder was jilted by the heavens when a day was by.

[*There is a distant noise of girls' voices. Widow Quin looks from window and comes to him, hurriedly*]

WIDOW QUIN You'll be doing like myself, I'm thinking, when I did destroy my man, for I'm above many's the day, odd times in great spirits, abroad in the sunshine, darning a stocking or stitching a shift; and odd times again looking out on the schooners, hookers, trawlers

is sailing the sea, and I thinking on the gallant hairy
fellows are drifting beyond, and myself long years
living alone.

CHRISTY [*Interested*] You're like me, so.

WIDOW QUIN I am your like, and it's for that I'm taking
a fancy to you, and I with my little houseen above
where there'd be myself to tend you, and none to ask
were you a murderer or what at all.

CHRISTY And what would I be doing if I left Pegeen?

WIDOW QUIN I've nice jobs you could be doing—gathering shells to make a whitewash for our hut within,
building up a little goose-house, or stretching a new
skin on an old curagh I have, and if my hut is far from
all sides, it's there you'll meet the wisest old men, I
tell you, at the corner of my wheel, and it's there yourself and me will have great times whispering and
hugging. . . .

VOICES [*Outside, calling far away*] Christy! Christy
Mahon! Christy!

CHRISTY : Is it Pegeen Mike?

WIDOW QUIN It's the young girls, I'm thinking, coming to
bring you to the sports below, and what is it you'll
have me to tell them now?

CHRISTY Aid me to win Pegeen. It's herself only that
I'm seeking now. [*Widow Quin gets up and goes to
window*] Aid me for to win her, and I'll be asking God
to stretch a hand to you in the hour of death, and lead
you short cuts through the Meadows of Ease, and up
the floor of heaven to the Footstool of the Virgin's
Son.

WIDOW QUIN There's praying!

VOICES [*Nearer*] Christy! Christy Mahon!

CHRISTY [*With agitation*] They're coming! Will you

84

swear to aid and save me, for the love of Christ?

WIDOW QUIN [*Looks at him for a moment*] If I aid you, will you swear to give me a right of way I want, and a mountainy ram, and a load of dung at Michaelmas, the time that you'll be master here?

CHRISTY I will, by the elements and stars of night.

WIDOW QUIN Then we'll not say a word of the old fellow, the way Pegeen won't know your story till the end of time.

CHRISTY And if he chances to return again?

WIDOW QUIN We'll swear he's a maniac, and not your da. I could take an oath I seen him raving on the sands today.

[*Girls run in*]

SUSAN Come on to the sports below. Pegeen says you're to come.

SARA TANSEY The lepping's beginning, and we've a jockey's suit to fit upon you for the mule race on the sands below.

HONOR Come on, will you?

CHRISTY I will then if Pegeen's beyond.

SARA She's in the boreen making game of Shaneen Keogh.

CHRISTY Then I'll be going to her now.

[*He runs out, followed by the girls*]

WIDOW QUIN Well, if the worst comes in the end of all, it'll be great game to see there's none to pity him but a widow woman, the like of me, has buried her children and destroyed her man.

[*She goes out*]   *only one who does show pity.*

CURTAIN

85

ACT III

Scene as before. Later in the day. Jimmy comes in, slightly drunk.

JIMMY [*Calls*] Pegeen! [*Crosses to inner door*] Pegeen Mike! [*Comes back again into the room*] Pegeen! [*Philly comes in in the same state—To Philly*] Did you see herself?

PHILLY I did not; but I sent Shawn Keogh with the ass-cart for to bear him home. [*Trying cupboards, which are locked*] Well, isn't he a nasty man to get into such staggers at a morning wake; and isn't herself the divil's daughter for locking, and she so fussy after that young gaffer, you might take your death with drouth and none to heed you?

JIMMY It's little wonder she'd be fussy, and he after bringing bankrupt ruin on the roulette man, and the trick-o'-the-loop man, and breaking the nose of the cockshot-man, and winning all in the sports below, racing, lepping, dancing, and the Lord knows what! He's right luck, I'm telling you.

PHILLY If he has, he'll be rightly hobbled yet, and he not able to say ten words without making a brag of the way he killed his father, and the great blow he hit with the loy.

JIMMY A man can't hang by his own informing, and his father should be rotten by now.

[*Old Mahon passes window slowly*]

PHILLY Supposing a man's digging spuds in that field with

86

a long spade, and supposing he flings up the two halves of that skull, what'll be said then in the papers and the courts of law?

JIMMY They'd say it was an old Dane, maybe, was drowned in the flood. [*Old Mahon comes in and sits down near door listening*] Did you never hear tell of the skulls they have in the city of Dublin, ranged out like blue jugs in a cabin of Connaught?

PHILLY And you believe that?

JIMMY [*Pugnaciously*] Didn't a lad see them and he after coming from harvesting in the Liverpool boat? 'They have them there,' says he, 'making a show of the great people there was one time walking the world. White skulls and black skulls and yellow skulls, and some with full teeth, and some haven't only but one.'

PHILLY It was no lie, maybe, for when I was a young lad there was a graveyard beyond the house with the remnants of a man who had thighs as long as your arm. He was a horrid man, I'm telling you, and there was many a fine Sunday I'd put him together for fun, and he with shiny bones, you wouldn't meet the like of these days in the cities of the world. some pass time

MAHON [*Getting up*] You wouldn't, is it? Lay your eyes on that skull, and tell me where and when there was another the like of it, is splintered only from the blow of a loy.

PHILLY Glory be to God! And who hit you at all?

MAHON [*Triumphantly*] It was my own son hit me. Would you believe that? happy that son clobbered him

JIMMY Well, there's wonders hidden in the heart of man!

PHILLY [*Suspiciously*] And what way was it done?

MAHON [*Wandering about the room*] I'm after walking hundreds and long scores of miles, winning clean beds

87

and the fill of my belly four times in the day, and I
doing nothing but telling stories of that naked truth.
[*He comes to them a little aggressively*] Give me a
supeen and I'll tell you now.

[*Widow Quin comes in and stands aghast behind
him. He is facing Jimmy and Philly, who are on
the left*]

JIMMY Ask herself beyond. She's the stuff hidden in her
shawl.   Carries her own brew

WIDOW QUIN [*Coming to Mahon quickly*] You here, is
it? You didn't go far at all?

MAHON I seen the coasting steamer passing, and I got a
drouth upon me and a cramping leg, so I said: 'The
divil go along with him,' and turned again. [*Looking under her shawl*] And let you give me a supeen,
for I'm destroyed travelling since Tuesday was a week.

WIDOW QUIN [*Getting a glass, in a cajoling tone*] Sit
down then by the fire and take your ease for a space.
You've a right to be destroyed indeed, with your walking, and fighting, and facing the sun. [*Giving him
poteen from a stone jar she has brought in*] There now
is a drink for you, and may it be to your happiness and
length of life.

MAHON [*Taking glass greedily, and sitting down by fire*]
God increase you!

WIDOW QUIN [*Taking men to the right stealthily*] Do you
know what? That man's raving from his wound today,
for I met him a while since telling a rambling tale of
a tinker had him destroyed. Then he heard of Christy's
deed, and he up and says it was his son had cracked his
skull. Oh, isn't madness a fright, for he'll go killing
someone yet, and he thinking it's the man has struck
him so?

trying to get rid of him

88

JIMMY [*Entirely convinced*] It's a fright surely. I knew a party was kicked in the head by a red mare, and he went killing horses a great while, till he eat the insides of a clock and died after.

PHILLY [*With suspicion*] Did he see Christy?

WIDOW QUIN He didn't. [*With a warning gesture*] Let you not be putting him in mind of him, or you'll be likely summoned if there's murder done. [*Looking round at Mahon*] Whisht! He's listening. Wait now till you hear me taking him easy and unravelling all. [*She goes to Mahon*] And what way are you feeling, mister? Are you in contentment now?

MAHON [*Slightly emotional from his drink*] I'm poorly only, for it's a hard story the way I'm left today, when it was I did tend him from his hour of birth, and he a dunce never reached his second book, the way he'd come from school, many's the day, with his legs lamed under him, and he blackened with his beatings like a tinker's ass. It's a hard story, I'm saying, the way some do have their next and nighest raising up a hand of murder on them, and some is lonesome getting their death with lamentation in the dead of night.

WIDOW QUIN [*Not knowing what to say*] To hear you talking so quiet, who'd know you were the same fellow we seen pass today?

MAHON I'm the same surely. The wrack and ruin of threescore years; and it's a terror to live that length, I tell you, and to have your sons going to the dogs against you, and you wore out scolding them, and skelping them, and God knows what.

PHILLY [*To Jimmy*] He's not raving. [*To Widow Quin*] Will you ask him what kind whas his son?

WIDOW QUIN [*To Mahon, with a peculiar look*] Was your

89

son that hit you a lad of one year and a score maybe,
a great hand at racing and lepping and licking the
world?

MAHON [*Turning on her with a roar of rage*] Didn't you
hear me say he was the fool of men, the way from
this out he'll know the orphan's lot, with old and
young making game of him, and they swearing, raging,
kicking at him like a mangy cur.

[*A great burst of cheering outside, some way off*]

MAHON [*Putting his hands to his ears*] What in the name
of God do they want roaring below?

WIDOW QUIN [*With the shade of a smile*] They're cheering
a young lad, the champion Playboy of the Western
World.

[*More cheering*]

MAHON [*Going to window*] It'd split my heart to hear
them, and I with pulses in my brain-pan for a week
gone by. Is it racing they are?

JIMMY [*Looking from door*] It is, then. They are mount-
ing him for the mule race will be run upon the sands.
That's the playboy on the winkered mule.

MAHON [*Puzzled*] That lad, is it? If you said it was a
fool he was, I'd have laid a mighty oath he was the
likeness of my wandering son. [*Uneasily, putting his
hand to his head*] Faith, I'm thinking I'll go walking
for to view the race.

WIDOW QUIN [*Stopping him, sharply*] You will not. You'd
best take the road to Belmullet, and not be dilly-
dallying in this place where there isn't a spot you
could sleep.

PHILLY [*Coming forward*] Don't mind her. Mount there
on the bench and you'll have a view of the whole.
They're hurrying before the tide will rise, and it'd be

near over if you went down the pathway through the crags below.

MAHON [*Mounts on bench, Widow Quin beside him*] That's a right view again the edge of the sea. They're coming now from the point. He's leading. Who is he at all?

WIDOW QUIN He's the champion of the world, I tell you, and there isn't a ha'p'orth isn't falling lucky to his hands today.

PHILLY [*Looking out, interested in the race*] Look at that. They're pressing him now.

JIMMY He'll win it yet.

PHILLY Take your time, Jimmy Farrell. It's too soon to say.

WIDOW QUIN [*Shouting*] Watch him taking the gate. There's riding.

JIMMY [*Cheering*] More power to the young lad!

MAHON He's passing the third.

JIMMY He'll lick them yet.

WIDOW QUIN He'd lick them if he was running races with a score itself.

MAHON Look at the mule he has, kicking the stars.

WIDOW QUIN There was a lep! [*Catching hold of Mahon in her excitement*] He's fallen? He's mounted again! Faith, he's passing them all!

JIMMY Look at him skelping her!

PHILLY And the mountain girls hooshing him on!

JIMMY It's the last turn! The post's cleared for them now!

MAHON Look at the narrow place. He'll be into the bogs! [*With a yell*] Good rider! He's through it again!

JIMMY He's neck and neck!

MAHON Good boy to him! Flames, but he's in!

[*Great cheering, in which all join*]

91

MAHON [*With hesitation*] What's that? They're raising him up. They're coming this way. [*With a roar of rage and astonishment*] It's Christy, by the stars of God! I'd know his way of spitting and he astride the moon.

[*He jumps down and makes a run for the door, but Widow Quin catches him and pulls him back*]

WIDOW QUIN Stay quiet, will you? That's not your son. [*To Jimmy*] Stop him, or you'll get a month for the abetting of manslaughter and be fined as well.

JIMMY I'll hold him.

MAHON [*Struggling*] Let me out! Let me out, the lot of you, till I have my vengeance on his head today.

WIDOW QUIN [*Shaking him, vehemently*] That's not your son. That's a man is going to make a marriage with the daughter of this house, a place with fine trade, with a licence, and with poteen too.

MAHON [*Amazed*] That man marrying a decent and a moneyed girl! Is it mad yous are? Is it in a crazy-house for females that I'm landed now?

WIDOW QUIN It's mad yourself is with the blow upon your head. That lad is the wonder of the western world.

MAHON I see it's my son.

WIDOW QUIN You seen that you're mad. [*Cheering outside*] Do you hear them cheering him in the zigzags of the road? Aren't you after saying that your son's a fool, and how would they be cheering a true idiot born?

MAHON [*Getting distressed*] It's maybe out of reason that that man's himself. [*Cheering again*] There's none surely will go cheering him. Oh, I'm raving with a madness that would fright the world! [*He sits down with his hand to his head*] There was one time I seen

ten scarlet divils letting on they'd cork my spirit in a
gallon can; and one time I seen rats as big as badgers
sucking the lifeblood from the butt of my lug; but
never till this day confused that dribbling idiot with
a likely man. I'm destroyed surely.

WIDOW QUIN And who'd wonder when it's your brain-
pan that is gaping now?

MAHON Then the blight of the sacred drouth upon myself
and him, for I never went mad to this day, and I not
three weeks with the Limerick girls drinking myself
silly and parlatic from the dusk to dawn. [*To Widow
Quin, suddenly*] Is my visage astray?

WIDOW QUIN It is, then. You're a sniggering maniac, a
child could see.

MAHON [*Getting up more cheerfully*] Then I'd best be
going to the union beyond, there'll be a welcome
before me, I tell you [*with great pride*], and I a terrible
and fearful case, the way that there I was one time,
screeching in a straightened waistcoat, with seven
doctors writing out my sayings in a printed book.
Would you believe that?

parellel to seven divils

WIDOW QUIN If you're a wonder itself, you'd best be hasty,
for them lads caught a maniac one time and pelted the
poor creature till he ran out, raving and foaming, and
was drowned in the sea. *horrible pleasures*

MAHON [*With philosophy*] It's true mankind is the divil
when your head's astray. Let me out now and I'll slip
down the boreen, and not see them so.

WIDOW QUIN [*Showing him out*] That's it. Run to the
right, and not a one will see.

[*He runs off*]

PHILLY [*Wisely*] You're at some gaming, Widow Quin;
but I'll walk after him and give him his dinner and a

time to rest, and I'll see then if he's raving or as sane as you.

WIDOW QUIN [*Annoyed*] If you go near that lad, let you be wary of your head, I'm saying. Didn't you hear him telling he was crazed at times?

PHILLY I heard him telling a power; and I'm thinking we'll have right sport before night will fall.

[*He goes out*]

JIMMY Well, Philly's a conceited and foolish man. How could that madman have his senses and his brain-pan slit? I'll go after them and see him turn on Philly now.

[*He goes; Widow Quin hides poteen behind counter. Then hubbub outside*]

VOICES There you are! Good jumper! Grand lepper! Darlint boy! He's the racer! Bear him on, will you!

[*Christy comes in, in jockey's dress, with Pegeen Mike, Sara, and other girls and men*]

PEGEEN [*To crowd*] Go on now, and don't destroy him, and he drenching with sweat. Go along, I'm saying, and have your tug-of-warring till he's dried his skin.

CROWD Here's his prizes! A bagpipes! A fiddle was played by a poet in the years gone by! A flat and three-thorned blackthorn would lick the scholars out of Dublin town!

CHRISTY [*Taking prizes from the men*] Thank you kindly, the lot of you. But you'd say it was little only I did this day if you'd seen me a while since striking my one single blow.

TOWN CRIER [*Outside ringing a bell*] Take notice, last event of this day! Tug-of-warring on the green below! Come on, the lot of you! Great achievements for all Mayo men!

PEGEEN Go on and leave him for to rest and dry. Go on,
I tell you, for he'll do no more.

[*She hustles crowd out; Widow Quin following
them*]

MEN [*Going*] Come on, then. Good luck for the while!

PEGEEN [*Radiantly, wiping his face with her shawl*] Well,
you're the lad, and you'll have great times from this
out when you could win that wealth of prizes, and
you sweating in the heat of noon!

CHRISTY [*Looking at her with delight*] I'll have great times
if I win the crowning prize I'm seeking now, and that's
your promise that you'll wed me in a fortnight, when
our banns is called.

PEGEEN [*Backing away from him*] You've right daring to
go ask me that, when all knows you'll be starting to
some girl in your own townland, when your father's
rotten in four months, or five.

CHRISTY [*Indignantly*] Starting from you, is it? [*He
follows her*] I will not, then, and when the airs is
warming, in four months or five, it's then yourself
and me should be pacing Neifin in the dews of night,
the times sweet smells do be rising, and you'd see
a little, shiny new moon, maybe sinking on the
hills.

PEGEEN [*Looking at him playfully*] And it's that kind of
a poacher's love you'd make, Christy Mahon, on the
sides of Neifin, when the night is down?

CHRISTY It's little you'll think if my love's a poacher's,
or an earl's itself, when you'll feel my two hands
stretched around you, and I squeezing kisses on your
puckered lips, till I'd feel a kind of pity for the Lord
God is all ages sitting lonesome in His golden chair.

PEGEEN That'll be right fun, Christy Mahon, and any girl

still testing him [handwritten annotation]

would walk her heart out before she'd meet a young man was your like for eloquence, or talk at all.

CHRISTY [*Encouraged*] Let you wait, to hear me talking, till we're astray in Erris, when Good Friday's by, drinking a sup from a well, and making mighty kisses with our wetted mouths, or gaming in a gap of sunshine, with yourself stretched back unto your necklace, in the flowers of the earth.

PEGEEN [*In a low voice, moved by his tone*] I'd be nice so, is it?

CHRISTY [*With rapture*] If the mitred bishops seen you that time, they'd be the like of the holy prophets, I'm thinking, do be straining the bars of paradise to lay eyes on the Lady Helen of Troy, and she abroad, pacing back and forward, with a nosegay in her golden shawl.

PEGEEN [*With real tenderness*] And what is it I have, Christy Mahon, to make me fitting entertainment for the like of you, that has such poet's talking, and such bravery of heart?

CHRISTY [*In a low voice*] Isn't there the light of seven heavens in your heart alone, the way you'll be an angel's lamp to me from this out, and I abroad in the darkness, spearing salmons in the Owen or the Carrowmore?

PEGEEN If I was your wife I'd be along with you those nights, Christy Mahon, the way you'd see I was a great hand at coaxing bailiffs, or coining funny nicknames for the stars of night.

CHRISTY You, is it? Taking your death in the hailstones, or in the fogs of dawn.

PEGEEN Yourself and me would shelter easy in a narrow bush [*with a qualm of dread*]; but we're only talking, maybe, for this would be a poor, thatched place to hold a fine lad is the like of you.

CHRISTY [*Putting his arm round her*] If I wasn't a good Christian, it's on my naked knees I'd be saying my prayers and paters to every jackstraw you have roofing your head, and every stony pebble is paving the laneway to your door.

PEGEEN [*Radiantly*] If that's the truth I'll be burning candles from this out to the miracles of God that have brought you from the south today, and I with my gowns bought ready, the way that I can wed you, and not wait at all. *Superficial love*

CHRISTY It's miracles, and that's the truth. Me there toiling a long while, and walking a long while, not knowing at all I was drawing all times nearer to this holy day.

PEGEEN And myself, a girl, was tempted often to go sailing the seas till I'd marry a Jew-man, with ten kegs of gold, and I not knowing at all there was the like of you drawing nearer, like the stars of God.

CHRISTY And to think I'm long years hearing women talking that talk, to all bloody fools, and this the first time I've heard the like of your voice talking sweetly for my own delight.

PEGEEN And to think it's me is talking sweetly, Christy Mahon, and I the fright of seven townlands for my biting tongue. Well, the heart's a wonder; and, I'm thinking, there won't be our like in Mayo, for gallant lovers, from this hour today. [*Drunken singing is heard outside*] There's my father coming from the wake, and when he's had his sleep we'll tell him, for he's peaceful then.

[*They separate*]

G   97

bring out best in each other

MICHAEL [*Singing outside*]

> The jailer and the turnkey
> They quickly ran us down,
> And brought us back as prisoners
> Once more to Cavan town

[*He comes in supported by Shawn*]

> There we lay bewailing
> All in a prison bound . . .

[*He sees Christy. Goes and shakes him drunkenly by the hand, while Pegeen and Shawn talk on the left*]

MICHAEL [*To Christy*] The blessing of God and the holy angels on your head, young fellow. I hear tell you're after winning all in the sports below; and wasn't it a shame I didn't bear you along with me to Kate Cassidy's wake, a fine, stout lad, the like of you, for you'd never see the match of it for flows of drink, the way when we sunk her bones at noonday in her narrow grave, there were five men, aye, and six men, stretched out retching speechless on the holy stones.

CHRISTY [*Uneasily, watching Pegeen*] Is that the truth?

MICHAEL It is, then; and aren't you a louty schemer to go burying your poor father unbeknownst when you'd a right to throw him on the crupper of a Kerry mule and drive him westwards, like holy Joseph in the days gone by, the way we could have given him a decent burial, and not have him rotting beyond, and not a Christian drinking a smart drop to the glory of his soul?

CHRISTY [*Gruffly*] It's well enough he's lying, for the likes of him.

MICHAEL [*Slapping him on the back*] Well, aren't you a hardened slayer? It'll be a poor thing for the house-

98

hold man where you go sniffing for a female wife; and [*pointing to Shawn*] look beyond at that shy and decent Christian I have chosen for my daughter's hand, and I after getting the gilded dispensation this day for to wed them now.

CHRISTY And you'll be wedding them this day, is it?

MICHAEL [*Drawing himself up*] Aye. Are you thinking, if I'm drunk itself, I'd leave my daughter living single with a little frisky rascal is the like of you?

PEGEEN [*Breaking away from Shawn*] Is it the truth the dispensation's come?

MICHAEL [*Triumphantly*] Father Reilly's after reading it in gallous Latin, and 'It's come in the nick of time,' says he; 'so I'll wed them in a hurry, dreading that young gaffer who'd capsize the stars.'

PEGEEN [*Fiercely*] He's missed his nick of time, for it's that lad, Christy Mahon, that I'm wedding now.

MICHAEL [*Loudly, with horror*] You'd be making him a son to me, and he wet and crusted with his father's blood?

PEGEEN Aye. Wouldn't it be a bitter thing for a girl to go marrying the like of Shaneen, and he a middling kind of a scarecrow, with no savagery or fine words in him at all?

MICHAEL [*Gasping and sinking on a chair*] Oh, aren't you a heathen daughter to go shaking the fat of my heart, and I swamped and drowned with the weight of drink? Would you have them turning on me the way that I'd be roaring to the dawn of day with the wind upon my heart? Have you not a word to aid me, Shaneen? Are you not jealous at all?

SHAWN [*In great misery*] I'd be afeard to be jealous of a man did slay his da.

99

PEGEEN Well, it'd be a poor thing to go marrying your like. I'm seeing there's a world of peril for an orphan girl, and isn't it a great blessing I didn't wed you before himself came walking from the west or south?

SHAWN It's a queer story you'd go picking a dirty tramp up from the highways of the world.

PEGEEN [Playfully] And you think you're a likely beau to go straying along with the shiny Sundays of the opening year, when it's sooner on a bullock's liver you'd put a poor girl thinking than on the lily or the rose?

SHAWN And have you no mind of my weight of passion, and the holy dispensation, and the drift of heifers I'm giving, and the golden ring?

PEGEEN I'm thinking you're too fine for the like of me, Shawn Keogh of Killakeen, and let you go off till you'd find a radiant lady with droves of bullocks on the plains of Meath, and herself bedizened in the diamond jewelleries of Pharaoh's ma. That'd be your match, Shaneen. So God save you now!

[She retreats behind Christy]

SHAWN Won't you hear me telling you . . . ?

CHRISTY [With ferocity] Take yourself from this, young fellow, or I'll maybe add a murder to my deeds today.

MICHAEL [Springing up with a shriek] Murder is it? Is it mad yous are? Would you go making murder in this place, and it piled with poteen for our drink tonight? Go on to the foreshore if it's fighting you want, where the rising tide will wash all traces from the memory of man.

[Pushing Shawn towards Christy]

SHAWN [Shaking himself free, and getting behind

Michael] I'll not fight him, Michael James. I'd liefer
live a bachelor, simmering in passions to the end of
time, than face a lepping savage the like of him has
descended from the Lord knows where. Strike him
yourself, Michael James, or you'll lose my drift of
heifers and my blue bull from Sneem.

MICHAEL Is it me fight him, when it's father-slaying he's
bred to now? [*Pushing Shawn*] Go on, you fool, and
fight him now.

SHAWN [*Coming forward a little*] Will I strike him with
my hand?

MICHAEL Take the loy is on your western side.

SHAWN I'd be afeard of the gallows if I struck with
that.

CHRISTY [*Taking up the loy*] Then I'll make you face
the gallows or quit off from this.

[*Shawn flies out of the door*]

CHRISTY Well, fine weather be after him [*going to
Michael, coaxingly*], and I'm thinking you wouldn't
wish to have that quaking blackguard in your house
at all. Let you give us your blessing and hear her swear
her faith to me, for I'm mounted on the spring-tide
of the stars of luck, the way it'll be good for any to
have me in the house.

PEGEEN [*At the other side of Michael*] Bless us now, for
I swear to God I'll wed him, and I'll not renege.

MICHAEL [*Standing up in the centre, holding on to both
of them*] It's the will of God, I'm thinking, that all
should win an easy or a cruel end, and it's the will
of God that all should rear up lengthy families for
the nurture of the earth. What's a single man, I ask
you, eating a bit in one house and drinking a sup in
another, and he with no place of his own, like an

old braying jackass strayed upon the rocks? [*To Christy*] It's many would be in dread to bring your like into their house for to end them, maybe, with a sudden end; but I'm a decent man of Ireland, and I liefer face the grave untimely and I seeing a score of grandsons growing up little gallant swearers by the name of God, than go peopling my bedside with puny weeds the like of what you'd breed, I'm thinking, out of Shaneen Keogh. [*He joins their hands*] A daring fellow is the jewel of the world, and a man did split his father's middle with a single clout should have the bravery of ten, so may God and Mary and St. Patrick bless you, and increase you from this mortal day.

CHRISTY *and* PEGEEN Amen, O Lord!

> [*Hubbub outside. Old Mahon rushes in, followed by all the crowd, and Widow Quin. He makes a rush at Christy, knocks him down, and begins to beat him*]

PEGEEN [*Dragging back his arm*] Stop that, will you? Who are you at all?

MAHON His father, God forgive me!

PEGEEN [*Drawing back*] Is it rose from the dead?

MAHON Do you think I look so easy quenched with the tap of a loy?

> [*Beats Christy again*]

PEGEEN [*Glaring at Christy*] And it's lies you told, letting on you had him slitted, and you nothing at all.

CHRISTY [*Catching Mahon's stick*] He's not my father. He's a raving maniac would scare the world. [*Pointing to Widow Quin*] Herself knows it is true.

CROWD You're fooling, Pegeen! The Widow Quin seen him this day, and you likely knew! You're a liar!

everyone against him

CHRISTY [*Dumbfounded*] It's himself was a liar, lying stretched out with an open head on him, letting on he was dead.

MAHON Weren't you off racing the hills before I got my breath with the start I had seeing you turn on me at all?

PEGEEN And to think of the coaxing glory we had given him, and he after doing nothing but hitting a soft blow and chasing northward in a sweat of fear. Quit off from this. *rejects him completely*

CHRISTY [*Piteously*] You've seen my doings this day, and let you save me from the old man; for why would you be in such a scorch of haste to spur me to destruction now? *good sense*

PEGEEN It's there your treachery is spurring me, till I'm hard set to think you're the one I'm after lacing in my heart-strings half an hour gone by. [*To Mahon*] Take him on from this, for I think bad the world should see me raging for a Munster liar, and the fool of men. *want revenge Torcher*

MAHON Rise up now to retribution, and come on with me.

CROWD [*Jeeringly*] There's the playboy! There's the lad thought he'd rule the roost in Mayo! Slate him now, mister.

CHRISTY [*Getting up in shy terror*] What is it drives you to torment me here, when I'd asked the thunders of the might of God to blast me if I ever did hurt to any saving only that one single blow.

MAHON [*Loudly*] If you didn't, you're a poor good-for-nothing, and isn't it by the like of you the sins of the whole world are committed?

CHRISTY [*Raising his hands*] In the name of the Almighty God . . .

MAHON Leave troubling the Lord God. Would you have Him sending down droughts, and fevers, and the old hen and the cholera morbus?

CHRISTY [*To Widow Quin*] Will you come between us and protect me now?

WIDOW QUIN I've tried a lot, God help me, and my share is done.

CHRISTY [*Looking round in desperation*] And I must go back into my torment is it, or run off like a vagabond straying through the unions with the dust of August making mudstains in the gullet of my throat; or the winds of March blowing on me till I'd take an oath I felt them making whistles of my ribs within?

SARA Ask Pegeen to aid you. Her like does often change.

CHRISTY I will not, then, for there's torment in the splendour of her like, and she a girl any moon of midnight would take pride to meet, facing southwards on the heaths of Keel. But what did I want crawling forward to scorch my understanding at her flaming brow?

PEGEEN [*To Mahon, vehemently, fearing she will break into tears*] Take him on from this or I'll set the young lads to destroy him here.

MAHON [*Going to him, shaking his stick*] Come on now if you wouldn't have the company to see you skelped.

PEGEEN [*Half laughing, through her tears*] That's it, now the world will see him pandied, and he an ugly liar was playing off the hero, and the fright of men.

CHRISTY [*To Mahon, very sharply*] Leave me go!

CROWD That's it. Now, Christy. If them two set fighting, it will lick the world.

MAHON [*Making a grab at Christy*] Come here to me.

CHRISTY [*More threateningly*] Leave me go, I'm saying.

104

MAHON I will, maybe, when your legs is limping, and your back is blue.

CROWD Keep it up, the two of you. I'll back the old one. Now the playboy.

CHRISTY [*In low and intense voice*] Shut your yelling, for if you're after making a mighty man of me this day by the power of a lie, you're setting me now to think if it's a poor thing to be lonesome it's worse, maybe, go mixing with the fools of earth. *complete fools*

[*Mahon makes a movement towards him*]

CHRISTY [*Almost shouting*] Keep off . . . lest I do show a blow unto the lot of you would set the guardian angels winking in the clouds above.

[*He swings round with a sudden rapid movement and picks up a loy*]

CROWD [*Half frightened, half amused*] He's going mad! Mind yourselves! Run from the idiot!

CHRISTY If I am an idiot, I'm after hearing my voice this day saying words would raise the top-knot on a poet in a merchant's town. I've won your racing, and your lepping, and . . . *discovered himself*

MAHON Shut your gullet and come on with me.

CHRISTY I'm going, but I'll stretch you first.

[*He runs at old Mahon with the loy, chases him out of the door, followed by crowd and Widow Quin. There is a great noise outside, then a yell, and dead silence for a moment. Christy comes in, half dazed, and goes to fire*]

WIDOW QUIN [*Coming in hurriedly, and going to him*] They're turning again you. Come on, or you'll be hanged, indeed. *killed his father ?*

CHRISTY I'm thinking from this out, Pegeen'll be giving me praises, the same as in the hours gone by.

good comment on whole play

WIDOW QUIN [*Impatiently*] Come by the back door. I'd think bad to have you stifled on the gallows tree.

CHRISTY [*Indignantly*] I will not, then. What good'd be my lifetime if I left Pegeen?

WIDOW QUIN Come on, and you'll be no worse than you were last night; and you with a double murder this time to be telling to the girls.

CHRISTY I'll not leave Pegeen Mike.

WIDOW QUIN [*Impatiently*] Isn't there the match of her in every parish public, from Binghamstown unto the plain of Meath? Come on, I tell you, and I'll find you finer sweethearts at each waning moon.

CHRISTY It's Pegeen I'm seeking only, and what'd I care if you brought me a drift of chosen females, standing in their shifts itself, maybe, from this place to the eastern world?

SARA [*Runs in, pulling off one of her petticoats*] They're going to hang him. [*Holding out petticoat and shawl*] Fit these upon him, and let him run off to the east.

WIDOW QUIN He's raving now; but we'll fit them on him, and I'll take him in the ferry to the Achill boat.

CHRISTY [*Struggling feebly*] Leave me go, will you? when I'm thinking of my luck today, for she will wed me surely, and I a proven hero in the end of all.

[*They try to fasten petticoat round him*]

WIDOW QUIN Take his left hand and we'll pull him now. Come on, young fellow.

CHRISTY [*Suddenly starting up*] You'll be taking me from her? You're jealous, is it, of her wedding me? Go on from this.

[*He snatches up a stool, and threatens them with it*]

WIDOW QUIN [*Going*] It's in the madhouse they should

good hearted

put him, not in jail, at all. We'll go by the back door to call the doctor, and we'll save him so.

[*She goes out, with Sara, through inner room. Men crowd in the doorway. Christy sits down again by the fire*]

MICHAEL [*In a terrified whisper*] Is the old lad killed surely?

PHILLY I'm after feeling the last gasps quitting his heart. [*They peer in at Christy*]

MICHAEL [*With a rope*] Look at the way he is. Twist a hangman's knot on it, and slip it over his head, while he's not minding at all.

PHILLY Let you take it, Shaneen. You're the soberest of all that's here.

SHAWN Is it me to go near him, and he the wickedest and worst with me? Let you take it, Pegeen Mike.

PEGEEN Come on, so. falls so low [*She goes forward with the others, and they drop the double hitch over his head*]

CHRISTY What ails you?

SHAWN [*Triumphantly, as they pull the rope tight on his arms*] Come on to the peelers, till they stretch you now.

CHRISTY Me!

MICHAEL If we took pity on you the Lord God would, maybe, bring us ruin from the law today, so you'd best come easy, for hanging is an easy and a speedy end.

CHRISTY I'll not stir. [*To Pegeen*] And what is it you'll say to me, and I after doing it this time in the face of all?

PEGEEN I'll say, a strange man is a marvel, with his mighty talk; but what's a squabble in your back yard, and the blow of a loy, have taught me that there's a great gap

107

between a gallous story and a dirty deed. [To men]
Take him on from this, or the lot of us will be likely
put on trial for his deed today.

CHRISTY [With horror in his voice] And it's yourself will
send me off, to have a horny-fingered hangman hitch-
ing slip-knots at the butt of my ear.

MEN [Pulling rope] Come on, will you?
[He is pulled down on the floor]

CHRISTY [Twisting his legs round the table] Cut the rope,
Pegeen, and I'll quit the lot of you, and live from this
out, like the madman of Keel, eating muck and green
weeds on the faces of the cliffs.

PEGEEN And leave us to hang, is it, for a saucy liar,
the like of you? [To men] Take him on, out
from this.

SHAWN Pull a twist on his neck, and squeeze him so.

PHILLY Twist yourself. Sure he cannot hurt you, if you
keep your distance from his teeth alone.

SHAWN I'm afeard of him. [To Pegeen] Lift a lighted
sod, will you, and scorch his leg.

PEGEEN [Blowing the fire with a bellows] Leave go now,
young fellow, or I'll scorch your shins.

CHRISTY You're blowing for to torture me. [His voice
rising and growing stronger] That's your kind, is it?
Then let the lot of you be wary, for, if I've to face the
gallows, I'll have a gay march down, I tell you, and
shed the blood of some of you before I die.

SHAWN [In terror] Keep a good hold, Philly. Be wary,
for the love of God. For I'm thinking he would liefest
wreak his pains on me.

CHRISTY [Almost gaily] If I do lay my hands on you, it's
the way you'll be at the fall of night, hanging as a
scarecrow for the fowls of hell. Ah, you'll have a

gallous jaunt, I'm saying, coaching out through limbo with my father's ghost.

SHAWN [*To Pegeen*] Make haste, will you? Oh, isn't he a holy terror, and isn't it true for Father Reilly, that all drink's a curse that has the lot of you so shaky and uncertain now?

CHRISTY If I can wring a neck among you, I'll have a royal judgment looking on the trembling jury in the courts of law. And won't there be crying out in Mayo the day I'm stretched upon the rope, with ladies in their silks and satins snivelling in their lacy kerchiefs, and they rhyming songs and ballads on the terror of my fate?

[*He squirms round on the floor and bites Shawn's leg*]

SHAWN [*Shrieking*] My leg's bit on me. He's the like of a mad dog, I'm thinking, the way that I will surely die.

CHRISTY [*Delighted with himself*] You will, then, the way you can shake out hell's flags of welcome for my coming in two weeks or three, for I'm thinking Satan hasn't many have killed their da in Kerry, and in Mayo too.

[*Old Mahon comes in behind on all fours and looks on unnoticed*]

MEN [*To Pegeen*] Bring the sod, will you?

PEGEEN [*Coming over*] God help him so.

[*Burns his leg*]

CHRISTY [*Kicking and screaming*] Oh, glory be to God!

[*He kicks loose from the table, and they all drag him towards the door*]

JIMMY [*Seeing old Mahon*] Will you look what's come in?

[*They all drop Christy and run left*]

CHRISTY [*Scrambling on his knees face to face with old*

Mahon] Are you coming to be killed a third time, or what ails you now?

MAHON For what is it they have you tied?

CHRISTY They're taking me to the peelers to have me hanged for slaying you.

MICHAEL [*Apologetically*] It is the will of God that all should guard their little cabins from the treachery of law, and what would my daughter be doing if I was ruined or was hanged itself?

MAHON [*Grimly, loosening Christy*] It's little I care if you put a bag on her back, and went picking cockles till the hour of death; but my son and myself will be going our own way, and we'll have great times from this out telling stories of the villainy of Mayo, and the fools is here. [*To Christy, who is freed*] Come on now.

CHRISTY Go with you, is it? I will then, like a gallant captain with his heathen slave. Go on now and I'll see you from this day stewing my oatmeal and washing my spuds, for I'm master of all fights from now. [*Pushing Mahon*] Go on, I'm saying.

MAHON Is it me?

CHRISTY Not a word out of you. Go on from this.

MAHON [*Walking out and looking back at Christy over his shoulder*] Glory be to God! [*With a broad smile*] I am crazy again. at last his son is a man [*Goes*]

CHRISTY Ten thousand blessings upon all that's here, for you've turned me a likely gaffer in the end of all, the way I'll go romancing through a romping lifetime from this hour to the dawning of the Judgment Day. [*He goes out*]

MICHAEL By the will of God, we'll have peace now for our drinks. Will you draw the porter, Pegeen?

SHAWN [*Going up to her*] It's a miracle Father Reilly can
  wed us in the end of all, and we'll have none to trouble
  us when his vicious bite is healed.

PEGEEN [*Hitting him a box on the ear*] Quit my sight.
  [*Putting her shawl over her head and breaking out into*
  wild lamentations] Oh, my grief, I've lost him surely.
  I've lost the only Playboy of the Western World.

poetic justice

can no longer be satisfied with shawn.

CURTAIN

Sara — shows human compassion

Philly — cynical, suspicious,

Shawn — nothing, weak
terribly fearful (dark nites
                    ghosts
                    Father Reilly)

— cruel + vicious
— material wealth

Widow Quinn — killed husband
                buried kids
    — individual strength
    — doesn't care about
           insults at her
    — compassion
    — best one yet most despised
    — like Christy for herself
           but helps him anyway.

113

Old Mahon - mistreated his son